21/20

Critical Guides to French Texts

47 Camus: L'Envers et l'Endroit *and* L'Exil et le Royaume

Critical Guides to French Texts

EDITED BY ROGER LITTLE, WOLFGANG VAN EMDEN, DAVID WILLIAMS

CAMUS

L'Envers et l'Endroit
and
L'Exil et le Royaume

Peter Dunwoodie

Senior Lecturer in French
Goldsmiths' College, London

Grant & Cutler Ltd
1985

I.S.B.N. 84-599-0481-4

DEPÓSITO LEGAL: V. 424 - 1985

Printed in Spain by
Artes Gráficas Soler, S.A., Valencia
for
GRANT & CUTLER LTD
11 BUCKINGHAM STREET, LONDON W.C.2

Contents

Contents

Prefatory Note

Editions referred to in this study are : *L'Envers et l'Endroit*, Gallimard, Collection 'Idées', and *L'Exil et le Royaume*, Gallimard 'Folio' paperback. Page numbers are given in parentheses in roman type. The following abbreviations have been used:

P1: A. Camus, *Théâtre, Récits, Nouvelles* (Bibliothèque de la Pléiade, 1967)
P2: A. Camus, *Essais* (Bibliothèque de la Pléiade, 1965)
*Carn.*I: *Carnets 1935-1942*
*Carn.*II: *Carnets 1942-1951*
*Cah.*I: *Cahiers Albert Camus,* I: *La Mort heureuse*
*Cah.*II: *Cahiers Albert Camus,* II: *Le Premier Camus.*

The figures in parentheses in italic type refer to numbered items in the Select Bibliography, usually followed by a page reference. In the bibliography I have listed most of the works dealing specifically with the two collections and a number of general works useful for further reading.

1. L'Envers et l'Endroit

Introduction

Published in Algiers when Camus was in his early twenties, the five short texts of *L'Envers et l'Endroit* (1937) are, on the author's own admission, among his most personal texts: 'la valeur de témoignage de ce petit livre est, pour moi, considérable [...] il exige une fidélité dont je suis seul à connaître la profondeur et les difficultés' (p.12). And yet, between 1937 and its republication in 1958, this collection was the least known of Camus's works, largely because the 350 copies of the first edition had long since disappeared. Consequently, for many critics, Camus's *œuvre* began with *Noces*, which is a much more joyous, 'pagan' celebration of life. Yet without the revelation of the darker side of Camus's sensibility, which *L'Envers et l'Endroit* provides, our image of the Camus of these years, on the threshold of his writing career, would remain incomplete and oversimplified, because the enjoyment of the world that he writes about is not a spontaneous, unthinking and uncomplicated pleasure-seeking. It is, on the contrary, permeated by a constant awareness of unhappiness, solitude, sickness and, above all, death. Camus's own experience of tuberculosis in 1930-31 left him deeply marked and gave him a physical awareness of ever-present death (see R. Quilliot, P2, p.1172), an awareness that must have reinforced the intellectual lessons he was learning in his study of philosophy, in his reading of Malraux, Montherlant, Grenier or Nietzsche.

L'Envers et l'Endroit is Camus's first published attempt to express the inner tension caused by the coexistence of this painful presence of death and his natural love of life, and in so far as the tension can be said to be controlled, this is achieved by a conscious intellectual effort to acknowledge both realities as essential and, more importantly, interdependent — as he indicates quite clearly in the *envers* and *endroit* image of the title. But the balance between the two poles, the joy of life and anguish in the face of death, is not in fact fully achieved here, as Camus acknowledged in a letter to his friend Jean de Maisonseul: 'Je lisais chez [les critiques] les mêmes phrases qui revenaient: amertume, pessimisme etc. Il n'ont pas compris [...]. Si je n'ai pas dit tout le goût que je trouve à la vie, si je n'ai pas dit que la mort même et la douleur ne faisaient qu'exaspérer en moi cette ambition de vivre, alors je n'ai rien dit' (P2, p.1219).

These pages do in fact often contain a note of almost injured grievance at what is seen as the 'injustice' of death; they are, on the whole, melancholic rather than passionate, sombre rather than illumined by the joys of life, for the anecdotic material they bring together is largely concentrated on unhappiness and alienation. The present analysis will therefore retrace the two poles which the title proclaims, their conflicts and their points of contact; we will follow the efforts of the author to remain always conscious of both, and the difficulties caused by this dualism.

The lyrical, reflective, largely autobiographical form adopted to fulfil this aim permits a tone of laconic detachment, an attitude of distance in the face of often bitter truths (see *1*, p.604). It allows Camus both to express deeply-felt personal emotions and to draw a number of general lessons from them, without either having to reconcile the antinomies which he had experienced or to lose the intimacy of personal involvement in the effort to find a literary transposition for them. His texts intertwine the lyrical and the logical, the immediacy of the concrete and the distance of the conceptual, in his first (published) attempt at transforming experience through language, and the conflict created by the unreconciled poles of the subject-matter is thus reflected directly (though, as we shall see, not always deliberately) in the tensions and uncertainties of a form which the mature artist of 1954 judged 'maladroite' (p.13). Indeed, the Camus of 1937 was both anxious about his powers of expression and conscious of a need to express: 'Après *L'Envers et l'Endroit* j'ai douté. J'ai voulu renoncer. Et puis une force de vie, éclatante, a voulu s'exprimer en moi: j'ai écrit *Noces*' (P2, p.1919).

Thus *L'Envers et l'Endroit* and *Noces* (1938) are to be situated on either side of the threshold into a new world, that of writing, of literature. In *Les Mots* Jean-Paul Sartre declared, 'je suis né de l'écriture' (Gallimard, Folio p.130), and the same can certainly be said of Camus who, in order to leave a world of silence (in which only his uncle read and owned books; P2, p.1117), has to choose in 1936-37 between two worlds, that of teaching — which he rejects in order to safeguard his freedom (see P1, p.xxxi; *29*, pp.47-76; and *31*, p.12) — and that of literature. Having chosen the world of the imagination, via literature, reality becomes merely the long list of jobs to earn a living, and writing becomes a choice of what he is to *be*, symbolising in his life a rejection of bourgeois, scholastic, repressive society. I should also mention two complicating factors, lest what precedes should appear too voluntaristic: firstly the effect of the tuberculosis which effectively blocked his path to the teaching qualification, *l'agrégation*; and secondly the problem of how, in the thirties, a working-class boy from a colonial background was able to gain entry to the (Paris) world of *belles lettres*.

Camus himself, however, always stressed his fidelity to his family background, indeed suggested that he saw writing as a means of expressing that fidelity (see P2, p.1117), and *L'Envers et l'Endroit* is his transformation of secret subjects, hidden desires, highly charged experiences and lessons learnt, which he can express once he has discovered that his working-class background can become a literary subject. It reveals part of the substance that Camus felt was present in every piece of writing, 'la part obscure, ce qu'il y a d'aveugle et d'instinctif' (P2, p.1925).

Finally, let me add that the importance of this collection lies not only in the fact that it presents a largely undisguised or untransposed, hence revealing, portrait of an artist in the making, his themes and images, his enthusiasms and reticences, but also in the practical contrast it provides with his last published work, *L'Exil et le Royaume* (1957), because this contrast will enable us to span the twenty years of Camus's *œuvre*, the often troubled path which he felt had taken him far from the atmosphere and the values expressed in *L'Envers et l'Endroit*: 'si j'ai beaucoup marché depuis ce livre, je n'ai pas tellement progressé. Souvent, croyant avancer, je reculais. Mais, à la fin, mes fautes, mes ignorances et mes fidélités m'ont toujours ramené sur cet ancien chemin que j'ai commencé d'ouvrir avec *L'Envers et l'Endroit*, dont on voit les traces dans tout ce que j'ai fait ensuite' (p.28).

The pages which follow analyse the themes of these five short texts, then the descriptive and narrative techniques employed. Throughout, I have tried to respect the independence of the narrator and of the text: I have therefore referred as little as possible to Camus's biography to 'explain' the texts and have rarely sought to identify Camus with the narrator(s).

Themes

Oscillating between positive and negative, joy and anguish, identification and detachment, Camus strains to express the interdependence of the two poles, *envers* and *endroit*, their inextricable and essential links; and they are to be read not alternately but simultaneously.

'Ironie' (for which much of the material is to be found in a 1934 text, 'Voix du quartier pauvre', *Cah.*I) sets the tone for the collection in a number of ways: thematically, it is dominated by old age and death yet asserts life and vitality; the world it depicts is that of Algeria and poverty; technically, it reflects not only the shifting relationship of the narrator to his material (sometimes observer, sometimes participant) but also his professed ironic attitude. I will deal here only with the thematic level.

The text consists of three short anecdotes: about a paralysed old woman 'réduite au silence et à l'immobilité' (p.35) when her family and the narrator go off to the cinema (p.38); an old man 'condamn[é] au silence et à la solitude' when young people in a café tire of listening to him talk about the past (p.43); a family which is dominated by a grandmother dismissed by the youngest child as a domineering comedienne, whose death is seen merely as a last performance. Such are the figures which, abandoned by the young, are also abandoned to their fate. And there is nothing reassuring about this fate (pp.40, 46), because the need for human warmth remains unfulfilled, and can indeed seem pathetically optimistic, for the human reality is bleak: not only because age is reduced to a depressing series of negative traits (the old woman's querulous fighting against the present, the old man's relentless repetition of stories from a past rendered falsely happy, the grandmother's deception and posturing), but because the deprivation of the old is not merely material but emotional and spiritual. Their dismal failure reinforces the irony of the fact that the young are busily engaged in trying to satisfy precisely the same needs (pp.38, 43), blind to the inevitable failure of such *divertissements* — which eventually only leave each individual 'livré tout entier à la pensée de la mort'.

The essential hopelessness of the situation here presented is, later, well encapsulated in the comment of the old Salamano (*L'Etranger*): '[la] vraie maladie, c'est la vieillesse, et la vieillesse ne se guérit pas' (P1, p.1158). The message put forward in the last few lines of 'Ironie' is explicitly isolated from the rest of the essay by a typographical break, a simple visual sign of the narrator's detachment from such pitiful figures, reinforcing his assertion that there is, 'de l'autre côté, toute la lumière du monde' (p.52).

'Entre oui et non' is an evocation of the role of memory and its influence on the present, a present in which the narrator is sitting alone at dusk in an Arab café and which is gradually covered by the past as natural echoes reawaken memories (pp.56, 58). The memories themselves are simple, unpretentious: a poor house and family; a night spent comforting a mother; a cat unable to feed her young; a (perhaps rare) visit to a mother. Sometimes lyrical, sometimes matter-of-fact, these memories are of the utmost importance because they reveal the emotional core of the experiences which Camus is evoking and transcribing in *L'Envers et l'Endroit*.

The first page points explicitly to both the adopted narrative attitude and the thematic centre of the entire collection: the acquired irony (proclaimed in the first essay) is silenced; the narrator (who sees himself as *émigrant*, *étranger*, a traveller returning) slowly rediscovers what he terms his *patrie*, in a series of *paradis perdus*, initially only vaguely described (p.55). The climactic experience undergone is made up of those few reminiscences, and through these a basic discovery appears (p.58), where the dominant feature is the awareness that he is living a privileged moment in which the flow of time seems to have been suspended. This is to be a recurrent theme: in the idea of paradise itself, of course; in his perception of the natural world as exuding 'l'indifférence et la tranquillité de ce qui ne meurt pas' (p.57); in his consciously accepting this experience as 'un intervalle entre oui et non' (p.68).

'La fille, infirme, pensait difficilement', 'Ironie' had said of the mother (p.47); 'Elle était infirme, pensait difficilement', repeats the second text (p.59). This suggests the fact that their ties are other than those formed via language and reason, indeed, it is her *mutisme* and *silence animal* which are singled out as the source of complex, barely understood emotions in the child as he stands silently looking at her sitting in the gathering darkness (p.61). This gives rise to a suffering which stems perhaps from his growing consciousness of his difference, of his mother's otherness, of their inevitable separation; yet the present moment of contemplation brings with it the consciousness of 'un temps d'arrêt, un instant démesuré', and the emotion which wells up is, 'dans l'élan qui l'habite, de l'amour pour sa mère' (p.61).

This positive note is, however, undermined in the second reminiscence which installs a disturbing parallelism between two occurrences: the evenings just described and a similar evening when the mother is attacked and the son has to spend the night with her. The parallels are quite explicit: her position in the room, the gathering darkness, her startled reaction; and some critics have seen this episode as the psychological centre of *L'Envers et l'Endroit* (see *23*, *26*), the climax of the chain of memories recalled by the narrator. In the silence which gradually envelops them he is aware of 'la peur du drame récent [qui] traînait dans la chambre sur-chauffée. [...] Dans l'air lourd flottait l'odeur du vinaigre dont on avait rafraîchi la malade' (pp.63-64). He feels *dépaysé*, echoing the introductory image of the *étranger* on the threshold of a lost paradise. In the illusory world which he imagines is crumbling around them he is left face to face with 'la maladie et la mort où il se sentait plongé', and the œdipal undertones produce fear and guilt at the infringement of a fundamental taboo: such an action destroys the natural order, symbolised by the figure of the Father thus overthrown, and the passage does indeed contain an acknowledgement of the destruction and of the symbolic achievement: 'Et pourtant, à l'heure même où *le monde croulait, lui vivait*. Et même il avait fini par s'endormir. Non cependant sans emporter l'image *désespérante et tendre* d'une solitude à deux' (p.65, my italics).

The symbolic transgression effected that night must be paid for, and Camus's works bear the trace of the turbulent emotions involved: recurrent elements such as a closed room, *peur*, *air lourd*, *odeur*... are always associated with anguish and death, for the old man of 'Ironie' (p.45), for the traveller in Prague (pp.81, 95), the death rooms of *La Peste* and, in particular, the *air lourd* at the death of Tarrou, in Clamence's fever and his room 'net[te] comme un cercueil' (P1, p.1538), in the *étrange odeur* which suffocates D'Arrast...

The oppressive physicality of this episode is soon replaced by an intricate pattern of intellectualised relationships and ideas built up around three terms which finally fuse the themes of mother and natural world as the repository of shared qualities and values: *indifférence*, *simplicité* and *transparence*.

'L'indifférence de cette mère étrange! Il n'y a que cette immense solitude du monde qui m'en donne la mesure' (p.63): by underlining this phrase Camus is able to highlight her silence and unexpressed love, and these become for the narrator the outward signs of her unfathomable *indifférence* which can only be compared to the vast self-sufficiency of the world in its absoluteness. It is this quality which he then returns to in a twice-repeated statement, inferring permanence or stasis (pp.66, 67), and once again mother and world *are* this reality: 'chaque fois qu'il m'a semblé éprouver le sens profond du monde, c'est sa simplicité qui m'a toujours bouleversé. Ma mère, ce soir, et son étrange indifférence' (p.66). The present moment is seen as an interval, time (change) suspended, as the narrator loses himself in the contemplation of 'la transparence et la simplicité des paradis perdus: dans une image' (p.68). This image is, yet again, that of the mother.

The intellectual distancing is, however, insufficient to harness the emotions involved, and the text continues with a more terrifying mother-figure in the passage on the cat which devours its last kitten in a room filled with 'l'odeur de mort et [...] d'urine' (p.67). The parallel with the night of the attack on his mother is made quite clear (p.65) and the way in which that episode leads without transition into the episode of the cat reveals how closely connected they are (p.66).

The final reminiscence (a visit by the son to his mother) again gives rise to an intellectual conclusion (pp.70-71) and is reinforced by a moral lesson, 'une indifférence sereine et primitive à tout et à moi-même' (p.71). Clearly, the function of both mother and world is to permit his withdrawal, into stasis, *indifférence*, that is into a loss of consciousness and desire, a fusing of the Self in the *Tout*. This is, in fact, a theme rarely absent from Camus's works, and it frequently appears as a temptation because it naturally deprives the individual of all-important lucidity (p.72).

The mother-son conversation actually prolongs the psychological resonances, not least because it provides a negative corollary to the key revelations linking mother and world: in this rare dialogue the figure of the father is evoked as an absence: 'Aucun souvenir, aucune émotion' on the part of the son, remembered only as the father of her children by the mother (pp.70, 60). This is psychologically advantageous in that it frees of any obstacle the son's exclusive relationship with the mother; and in later works the rigid, authoritarian attitudes of father figures (as tyrant or judge, for example) symbolise for Camus many of the bleak and destructive traits of contemporary society and history. By associating here (his father's) death for one's country and death imposed by the law, Camus attacks the facile euphemisms with which society surrounds capital punishment: it is not only death but, more specifically, its legalised, morally anaesthetised form (execution) that is omnipresent in Camus's *œuvre*.

If I have dwelt at length on these passages it is because in them we find an essential network: *monde, mère, silence, solitude, indifférence, transparence, mesure...* these terms are among the most fundamental in his writings, both emotionally charged and intellectually significant, signs of the roots of his experience and the source of his values. It is these pages which reveal his desire to 'édifier un langage et faire vivre des mythes' (p.31) by harnessing the energies of his own desires, fears and temptations (p.29).

'Entre oui et non' is a curiously mismanaged way to 'regarder [le] destin dans les yeux' (p.72) — the ideal which its conclusion proclaims. This journey into the past in order to be, at last, *rapatrié* through a conscious revival of the mother-son ties only unleashes the underlying psychological tensions, and 'La Mort dans l'âme' complements these with a more overtly disturbing dual journey in the present in which the narrator is gradually confronted with an overwhelming anguish which only Nature will allay. An account of a journey to Prague and Italy, 'La Mort dans l'âme' is also the account of an interior journey.

The canary-yellow lions and green-robed cheiks of 'Entre oui et non', forever frozen in hot pursuit and dramatically lit (p.57) evoked an impression of comforting bad taste and amateur theatricals. In contrast, the décor of 'La Mort dans l'âme' is immediately grimmer: the narrator is no longer spectator of his own past but an insecure actor in his present among bustling crowds (p.75). Not knowing the language or the way of life, hence unable to read the city around him, he is both lost and afraid, afraid above all of being reduced to solitude (pp.79, 80).

Such *divertissements* as the visiting of cultural landmarks remain inoperative because the narrator is increasingly conscious of an anguish which stems from the 'désaccord entre lui et les choses' (p.82). The lesson is forcefully, though a little theatrically, presented (p.83) in a phrase similar to the later description of the 'Absurd' awakening in *Le Mythe de Sisyphe* (P2, pp.106-07). He dismisses his own words as too emphatic, because the true lesson learnt is more frightening, because the experience is less easily controlled or defused by philosophising. He has gradually come face to face with the anguish provoked by an omnipresent 'odeur de vinaigre', and when language has failed, along with all his other resources, he is reduced to a humanly meaningless state: 'Je faisais mes ongles. Je comptais les rainures du parquet' (p.86). At this juncture the son is repeating the actions of the mother ('Entre oui et non', p.61) in an unconscious desire to repeat the past, to re-enact it, however symbolically, thus rejecting present consciousness and its newly laid-bare anguish.

Consequently, it is the town of his childhood and its summer evenings that he now remembers (*désespérément*, precisely because they cannot really be recaptured), a link immediately strengthened by a revealing admission which fuses past and present experiences: 'J'aurais pleuré comme un enfant si quelqu'un m'avait ouvert ses bras' (p.87). The arrival of his friends may fulfil the need here, but the solution is too weak to erase the memory of a lasting need left unfulfilled during his childhood: '[Sa mère] ne l'a jamais caressé puisqu'elle ne saurait pas' ('Entre oui et non', p.61). Here is, perhaps, the root of the fear and hostility which permeate the second text.

This *envers* is, however, counterbalanced in 'La Mort dans l'âme' by a positive corollary: Italy and, in particular, Vicenza provide the first detailed reference to *l'endroit*, that world which is both a basic fascination in Camus and an integral part of the antithesis which structures this collection. 'Terre faite à mon âme', writes Camus, 'tout m'est prétexte pour aimer sans mesure' (p.90), and the pages on Italy read like the reawakening of the senses after the anguished imprisonment of Prague, confessing the narrator's attachment to the pleasures of nature and 'la leçon du soleil et des pays qui m'ont vu naître' (p.92). This lesson is anchored in the constant tension: on the one hand the beauty and secret indifference of the natural world, on the other secret anguish and deep despair.

These positive lessons are repeated in 'Amour de vivre' (1936) which consists of evocations of three Italian scenes: it describes a Palma nightclub dancer, lyricises about the enforced lethargy in the midday streets, the moments of contemplative harmony experienced in the cloister of San Francisco at Fiesole, and the melancholy evenings on the port of Ibiza.

However divergent such episodes may at first sight seem, behind their variety lies a common emotion: of harmony, immediacy and vitality, of life's 'balance'. In them is stressed attentiveness, presentness, contemplation (pp.104, 108). The ideal, rarely attained, is complete depersonalisation, where he is 'porté [...] loin [...] de moi-même' (p.104), 'enlevé à moi-même' (p.106), lost in the present instant. Such moments clearly recall the *instant suspendu* which the son experienced close to his mother, moments of revelation not unlike the Joycean 'epiphany'.

The harmony which is attained remains, however, ephemeral (p.105), and if death is seen as the frighteningly inevitable future, life is at its most intense during these fleeting present moments. Clearly the physical nature of such experiences not only anchors them firmly in the world of the senses (constantly valorised) but, more centrally, points to the lesson that Camus is moving towards in this collection: man's sole reality is the present of this world, and his values, aims and ideals must be drawn from this reality, from within the acceptance of the life-death dichotomy which the title proclaims, from within its essential ambivalence.

This message is repeated in the title essay of the collection, 'L'Envers et l'Endroit' (probably 1937, although it uses *Carnet* material from January 1936; *Carn*.I pp.20-23): bringing together the various threads, it presents both an anecdote about others (like 'Ironie') and an autobiographical episode (like 'Entre oui et non'). It rewords the discovery written about in 'Amour de vivre' (p.116): *évanescence*, *impermanence*, *apparence*... The awareness conveyed is the same, and the extreme receptiveness of the narrator leads, as it had done in 'La Mort dans l'âme', to the formulation of a moral stance: 'Entre cet endroit et cet envers du monde, je ne veux pas choisir, je n'aime pas qu'on choisisse' (p.118). The two poles are thus once more maintained — and proclaimed — in their dynamic opposition and, far from searching for any kind of synthesis, Camus stresses the need to live within the tension they generate, because the love of life (perhaps somewhat intellectually?) is intensified by the accompanying despair at inevitable death (p.119).

In this way the reader is brought back to the attitude professed at the end of 'Ironie', pointing to the two major groups, or 'constellations', of themes which have been gradually unravelled here — those grouped around the pole of *l'envers* of the author's experience (old age, death, solitude, time and change); and the themes of *l'endroit* (nature, love, harmony, vitality and permanence). The surprising discovery lies in the fact that these themes are often conveyed by identical motifs: the closed room, silence, odours, the journey... an ambivalence essential to Camus's vision, in so far as both *l'envers* and *l'endroit* are ultimately necessary as interdependent moments of a dialectical relationship in which each enriches the other, because both are permanently present.

The dominant thematic movement of the collection is thus one of polarisation, via the continual interaction of past and present: on the one hand a constant 'retour aux sources', a harkening back to a lost *paradise* which can only be uncovered too late, which turns happiness into 'le sentiment apitoyé de notre malheur' (p.56), through consciousness of the permanent separation, exclusion. On the other hand, the 'epiphany' experienced in a momentary suspension of time is the ideal destination of the many journeys in the collection, journeys into the past or to the extremes of the Self, into the emptiness or the fullness of lived experience. Such notions continue to form endless variations on one basic, perhaps desperate movement (desperate since separation is always present): 'Si une angoisse encore m'étreint, c'est de sentir cet impalpable instant glisser entre mes doigts comme les perles du mercure' (p.117). The future can, of course, merely seal this separation.

It is within the shifting, polarised motifs used to formulate these discoveries that Camus situates the (also shifting) moral of his collection which, precisely because it relies for its emotional impact and its intellectual significance on a series of *unresolved* conflicts, cannot be neatly encapsulated in any single formula. It progresses from a preoccupation with happiness (p.56) to a focus on lucidity (pp.90, 103), and ends with the assertion: 'Ce n'est plus d'être heureux que je souhaite maintenant, mais seulement d'être conscient' (p.118). Such assertions seem almost to acquire the status of moral imperatives, especially in the references to lucidity, without which happiness would be merely illusory. It is again lucidity which dominates Camus's first major essay, *Le Mythe de Sisyphe* (1943).

Description

In a 1932 review of Bergson's *Les Deux Sources de la morale et de la religion* (P2, p.1207), Camus wrote: 'Rien de plus séduisant que cette idée: écarter l'intelligence comme dangereuse, baser tout un système sur la connaissance immédiate et les sensations à l'état brut'. His frequent attacks on the alienating effects of Reason indicate that this remained an ideal dear to Camus, for whom feelings hold more attraction than Reason. It is therefore important that we should look at *how* he gives a material, sensual density to the relationship between man and the world that this collection preaches.

Camus's attitude towards the natural world has been termed a 'sensual pantheism' (*30*, p.4); Camus himself acknowledged only a conscious avidity: 'que m'importe de mal étreindre si je peux tout embrasser' ('Amour de vivre', p.109). This prefigures the well-known ethic of quantity which *Le Mythe de Sisyphe* will later recommend (P2, pp.143-44). The attitude is of central importance since it is the absolute primacy of sense experience, of the body, which can alone guarantee the validity of Camus's early moral choice.

Not surprisingly for a North African writer, Camus's vision is heliocentric, and the lesson formulated is simple: 'Se nourrir de l'intensité du moment' (*Noces*). Consequently, in these pages Italy is described in terms of dryness: *tuiles écailleuses, cyprès grêle, murs crayeux, figuier poussiéreux, campagnes sèches*; and daylight is an *éblouissement* which leaves the narrator *chancelant*. More often, however, the presence of the sun is evoked as it were in the negative: in the *places pleines d'ombre* (pp.89, 104), in the play of light and shade — which constitutes the most prominent descriptive element throughout (pp.85, 89, 104, 115). The latter is important because it complements a stress on surfaces which, by playing down the density of objects, serves to underscore the theme of evanescence (pp.57, 65, 85, 92, 105, 115). The frequent recourse to verbs like *se défaire*, *se dissoudre*, *crouler*, *échapper* renders this surface fleetingness more dynamic, more dramatic.

The opposite effect is achieved in the frequent literary description of evening, sometimes dramatic (pp.59, 108), often calm and reflective in influence (pp.47, 57, 62, 91). In such description the sky is usually the focal point, with stars given special prominence, leading at times to quite baroque images (p.66). Such slow, peaceful rhythms are supported by descriptions which create an impression of a rich, atemporal present, hence of the physical permanence of the world. This is especially clear in the few cases where nominal sentences are used, as in the case of the cloister of San Francisco where Camus's description attains a transparency which reflects the pure, objective reality (pp.104-05). Such passages convey the impression of *moments suspendus*, stolen from the normal flux of time, moments in which the narrator disappears in the sensual contemplation of the natural world.

These visual descriptions are strengthened by a more physical though less dramatic tissue of olfactory impressions, which largely dominate the descriptions in *L'Envers et l'Endroit*: in the concrete description of a room (p.56), a town (pp.67, 69), the countryside (pp.89, 90, 91, 115), roasted coffee (p.62), cucumber or rosemary (pp.83, 89). More importantly, it is also a way of giving physical weight to abstract ideas, by linking for instance *mort* and *urine*, *ville* and *pouillerie*, *herbes* and *néant* (pp.67, 81). Smells are, indeed, sufficient to trigger an emotion, of anguish, enthusiasm or love (pp.65, 83, 93); and at times they generate fine examples of synesthesia which fuse in a long, sensual rhythm so many terms prominent in Camus's writing (pp.90-91).

'Tout mon royaume est de ce monde', proclaim the final lines (p.117), and a letter written shortly before the publication of *L'Envers et l'Endroit* expresses very directly the importance for Camus of surfaces, smells, shadows, silence or sunset, elements whose intangibility expresses the central theme of the collection, the nature of the kingdom: 'Qui suis-je d'autre que celui qui croit? Mais ce n'est pas à ce qui est derrière les parfums et les fleurs que je crois, c'est aux parfums et c'est aux fleurs. Et *c'est à l'apparence*' (P2, p.1173).

The intermingling of sense impressions, or the linking of sense impressions and abstract notions, blurs conventional, rational frontiers and forms the basis for the fusing of lived experience and philosophical lesson which structures the collection. They are signs of the narrator's links with the natural world, the ephemeral paradise which he declares his 'seul bien'. Yet they are also evidence of isolation, or at least separation, in so far as the use of the unexpected juxtaposition reflects the basic anti-theses which the title has installed as the thematic axis: *appel muet, aigre et tendre, désespérant et tendre, tendre et inhumain*... This ambivalence is clearly displayed in the water imagery used to build a picture of a dancer as a 'déesse immonde': the *filet jaune* of her costume is part of a realistic description of a noisy, drunken café scene, but it is also used to engender a positive metaphor through a series of simple modulations. Her body produces 'de petites *ondulations* de chair', from this 'de vraies *vagues* de chair naissaient', until finally, 'comme une déesse immonde sortant de l'eau [...] elle était comme l'image ignoble et exaltante de la vie' (p.102). Not an aesthetic Venus, but a grossly sexual symbol of life.

This contrasts with the more obviously intellectual extended metaphor which originates in the collection's title and takes two interlinked forms, both distancing the observer from such immediate, physical realities: *l'envers* and *l'endroit*, the right and wrong sides of a piece of cloth (p.116) and, by extension via 'le rideau des habitudes', a theatrical backdrop or décor (pp.82, 83, 102). The dualism contained in this central metaphor is proof that the author's vision is, in fact, only rarely depersonalised, fused with the reality he describes. There is, normally, a *distance* between them when the narrator acts as spectator, and it is this distance which permits the dominant mode used throughout, irony. The titles of both the collection and the first text and the juxtaposition of two contrasting titles ('La Mort dans l'âme'/'Amour de vivre') are all clear signals to the reader of how he is to approach these pages.

Irony is usually seen both as a mental attitude of the author and as a literary mode or rhetorical device (both relying on the reader's perception of the gap between literal content and intended message), and it is the former which is implied by Quilliot, for example, in a reference to Camus's 'propension à INTERROGER les apparences, cette lucidité corrosive qui s'attaque plus particulièrement aux faiblesses d'une chair que le temps marque insensiblement' (*31*, p.38).

This would clearly contradict the belief in appearances which Camus professed in the letter quoted earlier, but it is justified by the simultaneous presence of love and anguish, distance and communion, *envers* and *endroit* (see P2, p.1158). The linchpin of Camus's irony is consciousness of an essential dualism; his desire is neither blindly to believe in appearances, nor simply to question them; it is, as we have shown throughout, the urgent experience of both, without any illusion as to their incompatibility: 'J'entrais dans le jeu. Sans être dupe, je me prêtais aux apparences' (p.105). Just as awareness of death heightens man's pleasure in life, irony sharpens his consciousness, is in fact a vehicle for his lucidity (pp.108, 118), as Sisyphus was later to show (P2, p.196).

Yet irony has, for Camus, another function, which seems so far to have gone unnoticed by critics: it is clear that the distance and ironic detachment in the collection sometimes give way to enthusiasm, to lyrical passages, in short to displays of that subjectivity which Camus regretted; it therefore comes as no surprise to learn from a very early diary note (1933) that he also saw irony as a means of control: 'Il me faudrait apprendre à dompter ma sensibilité, trop prompte à déborder. Pour le cacher sous l'ironie et la froideur, je croyais être le maître. Il me faut déchanter' (*Cah.* II, p.201).

Thus, in *L'Envers et l'Endroit*, irony is both an intellectual guarantee of freedom (p.119) and a means of artistic control; it is the source of the dual significance of the descriptions, the antithetical themes and rhetorical devices.

Narration

In this collection all the texts deal with the lessons which Camus has drawn from a number of past experiences or instructive examples, and it will therefore be helpful to look at some of the methods used to integrate the past of the memories and the present of the narration which conveys the lesson.

It is the dual demands of autobiographical material and lyrical exposition which explain the dominant use of intercalated narration, that is to say a presentation in which the narrator's comments alternate throughout with the illustrative sequences. Three forms occur.

In 'Entre oui et non' the present of the narrator is made both temporally and spatially explicit (after two long paragraphs on the lost paradise revealed by retrospection), and this narrative situation ('ce soir, dans ce café maure', p.57) is returned to after each major flashback (pp.62, 65, 67, 71). In each case the transition between past and present is clearly marked by changes of tense, while the sequences have a chronological relationship which, though distancing the narrator, reinforces the complex lessons to be learned. The text ends with the fusing of the two moments as the reminiscences become a conscious part of the narrator's present (p.71).

The form used in 'La Mort dans l'âme' takes this a step further by integrating a more obvious antithetical structure, spatial and thematic, and by direct personal involvement of the narrator. The two opposed sequences, Prague and Italy, are introduced by similar terms (pp.75, 89), and their introductory present tenses are soon replaced by past tenses, via clear transitions which refer to the moment of composition: 'Je me demande, encore aujourd'hui[...]' (p.79), 'c'est maintenant seulement[...]' (p.92).

The third technique used to provide a past-present contrast is a text-within-a-text, written during the narrator's stay in Prague. It both illustrates his state of mind at the time and allows a critique thereof, for by condemning his text when introducing it and by ending with a dismissive 'c'étaient des histoires pour m'endormir' (p.83), the distance between the two moments is highlighted and his present heightened lucidity is implied. Similarly, the final paragraph ensures that present awareness predominates by blending the two sequences in the image of the little cemetery overlooking the bay (p.95): Prague, anguish, death ... Italy, happiness, vitality, nature. In this way the implication is, once more, that the narrator's present consciousness of the coincidence or the simultaneity of these two poles is the sole positive conclusion.

The form given to 'L'Envers et l'Endroit' reasserts the importance of this heightened present consciousness: a present-tense narration is used to give prominence to a present state of mind and personal involvement. Since this both brings the collection to an end and recalls the general title it would seem to carry the weight of Camus's summing up; and with it the whole collection is anchored firmly in the present through repeated reference to the increasingly contemporaneous moment of narration (p.116).

The narrative techniques thus continually emphasise this 'presentness' as the direct result of the 'recherche du temps perdu' undertaken by the narrator — and of which the closed room, hidden in the past, is the emotional core. They are therefore not merely formal literary devices, but the expression of precisely that awareness which forms the thematic centre and explicit lesson of the collection: the aggressive assertion of the unique value of the present.

The second major narrative characteristic to note is the direct intervention of the narrative 'I' — which, as a letter from Camus to Jean de Maisonseul in July 1937 acknowledges, reveals the autobiographical nature of much of the material: 'il fallait rester dans la coulisse. Mais d'abord je manque de métier et ces résonances qui me sont si sensibles [...] c'est ma jeunesse et mon amour de vivre qui m'empêchent de les rendre objectivement' (P2, p.1218). Far from being objective, both first- and third-person sequences are permeated by that narrative voice.

'Ironie' is evidence of Camus's uncertainty here, since three attitudes coexist in these few pages: the intervention of the narrator is at times unconscious and discreet (compare the behaviorism of 'il paraissait bien que ce geste pouvait être[...]'

with the omniscience of 'Elle sentait déjà l'horreur de sa solitude', p.39); at other times it is conscious but somewhat disruptive (as in the very odd 'Je l'ai vu. C'est ridicule, mais qu'y faire', p.45). Elsewhere it can be justified by the moralising, and hence generalising, aim (as in 'le soleil nous chauffe quand même les os', p.52).

'La Mort dans l'âme' and 'Amour de vivre' best illustrate the first-person sequences: in the first the narrator's interventions refer predominantly to problems of artistic expression and they can be seemingly vacuous (in so far as they add no new information), a rather facile rhetorical padding, as in 'Mais vais-je décrire les jours qui suivirent?' (p.79); or they can deal with the rhetoric of writing (pp.81, 83, 88). Finally, they can function as indicators of the difficulty of expressing the inexpressible, in order no doubt to enhance its mystery: 'Mais c'était l'angoisse de Prague et ce n'était pas elle. Comment l'expliquer' (p.93). In 'Amour de vivre', on the other hand, the focus of such interventions — with their inescapable hint of artificiality — is less on writing than on the process of rethinking past experiences (pp.104, 105, 106).

It is probable that such variety in the functions of the narrative 'I' is, as Camus recognised, partly the result of technical uncertainty. Yet they are revealing in that they reflect the tensions of the past/present dichotomy in the form reminiscence/expression, as well as the difficult process of combining the two in a new awareness, especially if recapturing the hidden, secret and deeply significant elements of lived experience is more revealing and more demanding than the presentation of impersonal, intellectualised episodes — which often owe a great deal to a literary and philosophical subtext.

Conclusion

The seeds of Camus's *œuvre* are now visible in *L'Envers et l'Endroit*. Some of these his subsequent texts will bring to fruition; others, and not the least important, will at times be crowded out by more bitter realities. A brief summary of those major themes and techniques may therefore help us project them forwards, across the works which followed, to the period of *L'Exil et le Royaume*.

1. The necessary dialectical relationship between love of life and awareness of death, the harmony or fusion which is man's desire forever linked to the injustice of separation which is his destiny.

2. The interwoven strands, mother — world — son, locked in exceptionally exclusive ties (mother and son share 'une solitude à deux' and nowhere is the experience of harmony with Nature shared with others). The values embodied in mother and world are both essential (if individual life in the world is to achieve harmony) and problematic (if individual life in human society is to be made meaningful).

3. The psychological and artistic *retours* which give the collection i) its distinctive tone of nostalgia disguised by irony, ii) its central images of *voyage* and *rapatriement*, iii) its technique of retrospection through flashback.

4. The exceptional stress on the unique value of the present.

5. The gradual displacement of the theme of happiness by that of lucidity, which is prominent, variously disguised, in all the subsequent texts.

In an introduction to *L'Exil et le Royaume* Camus wrote of 'une certaine vie libre et nue que nous avons à retrouver pour renaître enfin' (P1, p.2039), and it is to that collection that we must now turn our attention. The question implicit throughout will be whether these short stories are a final *retour*, the rewritten *L'Envers et l'Endroit* which Camus admitted was his aim (in the preface to the republication of the volume in 1954). How faithful has he been to the vision and aesthetic of this early collection? How many changes have the intervening twenty years forced upon him?

2. L'Exil et le Royaume

Introduction

L'Exil et le Royaume consists of six stories written between 1952 and 1955, first published under this collective title in 1957 — a title which, in its two-part structure juxtaposing negative and positive poles, is clearly reminiscent of *L'Envers et l'Endroit*.

The stories describe a number of very diverse lives: from a rather passive housewife to a violently apostate missionary, from the routine activity of a group of working men to the *dépaysement* of a civil engineer newly arrived in Brazil, or the creative anxieties of a Parisian artist. The individual portraits explore a cross-section of society as wide as that of *La Peste* for instance, yet by isolating each within the confines of its own story Camus no longer needs a factor like the plague which will englobe them all: all are exiled, but each lives out his or her own form of exile. In this respect the choice of the short story can be seen as more radical than the chronicle form given to *La Peste*, because fragmentation, isolation and lack of any continuity are more concretely, more formally expressed here than in the novel, which necessarily forms its own microcosm: each is exiled, but all are exiled together.

The short story as genre has been the subject of a great deal of critical work, so I will do no more here than enumerate some of its major characteristics. To begin with the most obvious: a short story implies a compactness of form and a limit to the amount of material which can be included. Consequently, description, psychological analysis and social information are, of necessity, used economically, often by restricting them to the purely personal viewpoint of the protagonist and the limits of his experience. On the narrative level, two major approaches are common: firstly a single situation can be developed, often covering no more than a few hours or days in the life of the hero and, through rapid stages, leading to the working out of a conflict, a crisis (it is sometimes suggested that a whole story can stem from a single, critical final sentence or gesture, as in the *solitaire/solidaire* ending of 'Jonas' for example). In the present collection 'La Femme adultère', 'Les Muets', 'L'Hôte' and 'La Pierre qui pousse' cover a period of 24 hours or a little more; time passing and chronology are much in evidence, and a few clearly-marked flashbacks provide necessary information and insights; the focus is squarely on concrete actions and individual events, building up inexorably from the beginning and leading through shifts in the hero's awareness, to the moment of revelation. Hence the term 'epiphanic' often applied to this type of story.

The second narrative approach produces stories which can be temporally rather ill-defined, which cover a much longer period in the life of the protagonist. To do this they most often resort to summary and condensation (of childhood, travels, success), with the accent on becoming, on evolution or *déroulement* (rather than on the moment of crisis or *dénouement*). In both 'Le Renégat' and 'Jonas' the actions are of little significance since the focus is on an overview of the past and the protagonists' evolution rather than on the presentation of a picture of their present. Here the chronology is less clear, and flashbacks play a much smaller part, since it is the entire story which deals with the retelling of their past. The present thus appears as a consequence of the past rather than as a moment of discovery.

Each of the stories is focussed on one central character and, with the exception of 'Le Renégat', the most dominant feature of their psychology is a consciousness of alienation harnessed to an ideal of harmony: Camus writes of 'un seul thème [...] celui de l'exil' (P1, p.2039), and the fact that the collection's title (which points directly to the theme to be explored) does not also belong to any one story suggests that it functions as a unifying principle, tying together the multiple strands (of the individual lives) and linking them through key terms and images.

The 'Prière d'insérer' talks mainly about technique, about a theme which is 'traité de six façons différentes, depuis le monologue intérieur jusqu'au récit réaliste', and it is true that diversity is the most striking feature of these stories: in technique, from realism ('Les Muets') to expressionism ('Le Renégat'), from traditional narration ('La Femme adultère') to internal monologue ('Le Renégat'); in tone, from lyricism to the ironic and legendary. Consequently, it is this aspect which will come frequently to the fore in the pages which follow, through the analysis firstly of the individual stories, then of their links in the light of the collection's title, and finally when comparing and contrasting the collection with *L'Envers et l'Endroit*.

'La Femme adultère'

The opening paragraphs have a triple function: they constitute a starkly realistic description of the occupants of a bus crossing the high plateaux of the Algerian south; they contain a summary of the major themes which the story is to develop in a series of oppositions (imprisonment vs. freedom, awareness vs. unconsciousness, passive acceptance vs. choice); and finally, they set in motion the central evolution of the heroine, Janine, from absence (as a woman circumscribed and summarised by her relations with others) to presence (as a woman experiencing a conscious fusion of body, mind and cosmos).

A thin, exhausted fly is caught within the hostile, confined space of a bus which is itself buffeted by wind and sand. Watching its flight the onlooker, Janine, is made conscious of her husband's presence, a heavy passivity which dominates his physical characteristics, more a body next to Janine's than someone she actually looks at.

No personal reaction or judgement by the onlooker is implied, indeed it remains quite neutral until the silence and immobility of her fellow-travellers are noted (p.12). Until then she had been only a gaze noting whatever attracted her attention, really no less passive than her husband and actually more absent: looked at by a soldier her reaction is to see herself as the (passive) object of desire (p.14), and later her absence is highlighted (pp.18, 25). Only at the end of the story, when she is no longer dependent on others, no longer weighed down by them, when she finally dares abandon her husband, does she become the subject of her own actions, having opened her eyes to her own life.

The symbolism of the opening paragraphs can be seen to encapsulate the major factors of her initial state and her final liberation: the long imprisonment of her life of 25 years within the walls of their little flat (p.15), which has slowly cut her off from the world of sand and sea; her unnoticed presence as Marcel is increasingly absorbed in his business (symbolised by the 'mallette d'échantillons' and their attitudes towards it); her growing heaviness which cuts her off from a past in which she was light and agile. It is from all these that she flees in a 'course folle', a 'dernier élan' which thrusts her into the forefront of her own life, makes her once again the author of her own actions.

The path towards this liberating rediscovery of the Self and the world is the path to Janine's kingdom, and it develops through four stages which are clearly marked temporally, spatially and psychologically: the morning bus trip and reflections on a restricted married life; the arrival at the oasis town, which provides some protection and a glimpse of the outside world, causing a daydream of lost youth; the sales efforts, the visit to the fort when the desert vastness overwhelms the heroine; Janine's return to the fort during the night. In each phase the desert world parallels the landscapes of the heroine's mind, climaxing in the final mysterious fusing of the two.

This relationship is made quite clear in the first phase, revealed through the motif of the journey which, as Camus wrote in 'La Mort dans l'âme', triggers off a 'voyage intérieur' by stripping the traveller of his defences and bringing him face to face with the world (p.34). This process brings Janine the growing awareness of an alienation which is racial, emotional and sexual in its direct manifestations (pp.14, 25). Her uneasiness is first aroused by the outside world, the hostile, inhospitable world of the Algerian south, which is presented through a number of anthropomorphic images (pp.12, 17) and described as bearing only metallic palm-trees, dry plants among sand and stone (pp.12, 13, 16, 21). This hostility is complemented by a prolonged spatial metaphor of confinement (pp.12, 18) which may be seen as a symbol of the heroine's imprisonment within a closed existence, for Janine's account of her marriage describes it in terms of a gradual narrowing and emotional shrinking of their life together, once all needs have been reduced to economic ones, once tenderness has been replaced by money and objects (p.15). It is this microcosm of the stuffy petty-bourgeois mix of statutary folk art ('tentures arabes') and the tasteless mass-produced ('meubles Barbès') which clashes with the emptiness of the Arab world which surrounds them. Even Marcel's central desire implies confinement: 'S'il m'arrivait quelque chose [...] tu serais à l'abri' (p.15).

Both Janine and Marcel are physically heavy individuals, and this trait is seen as a major point of contrast with those around her, whether the soldier (p.14) or the Arabs: the weight, the clumsiness, the unease are all given precise physical causes in the first phase, and they combine in the second to defeat the heroine when she enters the hotel room which, far from being the hoped-for haven from sand and cold, is only another dispiriting, hostile environment (p.19). The desert, the bus, the storm, the hotel room, whether or not we wish to read them symbolically as concrete manifestations of a Clamence-type 'malconfort', are at the very least realities which shatter the heroine's secure décor, leaving her unprotected. As she left the bus description and psychological insight into character had been linked (p.18) and now, when physically most defeated, the palm-trees she had glimpsed trigger off a revealing daydream: 'Elle rêvait aux palmiers droits et flexibles, et à la jeune fille qu'elle avait été' (p.20). Her earlier nostalgia for the physical gracefulness of youth fuses with the present image and the harsh metaphors based on dryness, hardness and metal are replaced by water images suggesting gentleness (pp.19, 20). This contrast of images mirrors the conflict of an irretrievable past and an imagined solace in the present, dream and reality (pp.19-20).

This daydream forms the initial positive response to the impact of the desert world, at the moment when the heroine is alone for the first time and the focus is solely on her. Janine is now clearly the subject of the story, and her psychological state is one of expectancy (pp.19, 15). She is, in other words, still

essentially passive psychologically, though now more central to
the narrative development.

Lunch provides more realistic explanations for her uneasiness
(p.21) with a precision highly unusual in Camus's texts, and
which has led numerous critics to stress the realism evident in
many of these stories (see P1, p.2040 and *9*, p.17). This realism
is much in evidence throughout the third phase of the story,
since the afternoon episode begins with an account of Marcel's
sales efforts and, in particular, with the detailed description of
the interior of an Arab shop (pp.21-22). In this episode Janine is
again displaced as actor, becoming merely the involuntary
witness of Marcel's action and noting, as though objectively, his
insecurity both vis-à-vis his customers and the Arab soldier who
ignores them (pp.22, 24). The exclusion of the heroine is discreetly referred to (pp.22, 23); her presence is unimportant until
she finally expresses a desire, to go to the fort: 'Il la regarda,
soudain attentif' (p.24).

We are shown throughout this episode that the heroine is
increasingly aware of her alienation and this is articulated as a
repeated desire to escape. Meanwhile, her physical discomfort,
her inability to read the Arab world around her, increase her
feeling of insecurity (pp.24, 25). In a context which echoes the
opening paragraphs of 'La Mort dans l'âme' the heroine is seen
as defenceless, especially as her recourse to memory (p.24)
merely aggravates her present discouragement. While the highly
self-conscious narrator of the essay in *L'Envers et l'Endroit*
could talk (indeed, sit in his hotel room and write) of despair,
the advantages (psychological and philosophical) of travel etc.,
Janine, less analytic and less articulate, sees her malaise in
physical terms, in heaviness, whiteness, even indigestion (pp.21,
22, 25).

It is, however, *her* decision to go and 'see the desert' (p.24),
and although this is obviously another expression of her need to
escape, albeit temporarily, it is also the first point in the
heroine's evolution where her desire initiates an action rather
than merely responding to others.

The salient feature of the episode on the fort lies in its use of
terms directly opposed to the major elements of the first two

phases: the closing and cluttering up of her past life, the imprisonment imposed by the sandstorm, give way to the opening out of space and a beginning of liberation in the physical opening-out of a sky at last 'tout entier découvert', through a network of metaphors which fuse space, light and sound, in which the heroine's perception is noted as it takes in the space around her (pp.25-26). Perceiving 'une étrange écriture dont il fallait déchiffrer le sens', the heroine is conscious, through a continued focus of spatial elements, of the desert vastness which reveals a new fact: 'ce royaume, de tout temps, lui avait été promis [...] et jamais, pourtant, il ne serait le sien, plus jamais, sinon à ce fugitif instant, peut-être' (p.27).

Two facts underline the importance of this moment: firstly the repetition of the *royaume* of the collection's title, and secondly the use of a vocabulary and an imagery which imply the increased presence of the narrator since the text abandons the limitations imposed by Janine's mental and linguistic capacities. The claustrophobic world of the past has opened out onto a present kingdom, and it is this discovery which the narrative shift stresses while keeping it within the framework created for the heroine: the opening pages had revealed some of her deepest fears and the climax of the episode is related to this: 'Il lui sembla que le cours du monde venait alors de s'arrêter et que personne, à partir de cet instant, *ne vieillirait plus ni ne mourrait*' (p.28, my italics).

The episode ends with the reintroduction of movement and sound, but it is clear that the situation has now changed dramatically, for the heroine has reached a new state of desire and awareness. Yet she continues to feel excluded, once the moment of exaltation has passed. It is at this point in the narrative that the figures encountered earlier acquire their full significance, as the sole rightful inhabitants of this world. The experience thus brings to a head conflicts latent in the heroine's past and heralds a possible future path: it is as 'la jeune fille qu'elle avait été' (p.20) that Janine could bring her exile to an end by casting off the passivity and emotional impoverishment that 25 years of sheltered marriage had brought. Meanwhile, she is subjected to fear and fever, a growing malaise.

In the fourth and final stage of the story anguish actually overwhelms the heroine as she dissects her relationship with Marcel and acknowledges a number of judgements and conclusions hitherto seemingly glimpsed but not voiced: picking up the thread of her earlier 'Non, elle n'était pas seule' (p.13), she sees their ties as based on a need for protection against solitude in old age and the fear of death (p.31). In this she is once again in an essentially passive position, of course, since it is Marcel who, in reality, finds in her this protection, and a manuscript passage makes more explicit what the published text suggests: '[les] hommes qui ont peur de mourir et qui masquent avec un corps de femme ce que la solitude et la mort leur montrent d'effrayant et qui veulent désespérément parfois ce corps pour oublier l'angoisse de vivre' (P1, p.2042). In this the woman is a means, not a subject.

Here, the couple are deprived of even this Pascalian *divertissement*, because their relationship is actually desexualised, for despite her knowing herself to be 'charnelle, et encore désirable' (p.14) — and the function of the soldier in the text was to call this to the reader's attention — Janine's role in the couple has become largely maternal (p.31). It is this weakness in Marcel, no doubt, which gives a retrospective explanation of the ambiguity inherent in his sales technique (p.22) and his meek submission when dismissively treated by 'un grand Arabe, maigre, vigoureux' (p.23).

The climax of Janine's introspection (which constitutes the decisive psychological moment of the narrative) occurs precisely when she finally recognises that their life together adds to her malaise: she awakens totally unprotected and her past disintegrates in an instant as she discovers herself alienated from the past and within the present, conscious of the urgency of the exceptional moment (*aussitôt*, *soudain*, *maintenant*, *à l'instant*).

Analysis of the last episode reveals that it completes this fundamental experience, initiated during the afternoon visit to the fort, for close parallels exist between the two in both the overall movement and in the language used, leading to the anticlimactic 'ce n'est rien' which, as in the earlier 'tu es stupide. Rentrons' (p.28), stresses the return to normality.

In contrast to the earlier episode, however, the night-time passage is heavily sexualised (see P1, p.2040). The 'adultery' is both a mystical moment and an erotic experience and, as such, is a rare passage in Camus's *œuvre*; it clearly recalls the sensuality of *Noces* and its focus on the night sky, through a network of metaphorical terms centred on the stars, is reminiscent of numerous references in *L'Envers et l'Endroit*. It is only when the movement of the stars comes to an end that the other dominant element, the cold, is finally defeated and the experience reaches its climax.

This is accompanied by the evocation of a more turbulent inner struggle (which also echoes the afternoon episode), and it is in the sentence which concludes the movement of the natural elements that the heroine's fusion with the world is finally achieved; 'l'eau de la nuit' is in both Janine and the cosmos (p.34).

Solitude, silence and immobility accompany this fusion, less in the suspension of time and movement experienced earlier than in a much more mysterious 'sorte de giration pesante' and 'cheminement immobile', in harmony with the movement of the stars. The momentary halt in the flux of the natural order (in the earlier episode) left the underlying antithesis unchanged: permanence (immobility) in the present vs. change (movement) in time. Here, on the contrary, the oxymoron 'cheminement immobile' transcends the opposition, fuses the two terms and suggests that mystical unity of the Self and the world which Camus's early texts had, at times, evoked.

The basic desirability and inexpressibility of the experience shows in the writing: across a hiatus of 25 years ('elle oubliait') Janine rediscovers the vitality of a young girl (*retrouver, à nouveau*), and it is this young girl who can share the kingdom of the desert. Her orgasmic experience is thus both a fusion with the natural world and a rediscovery of the Self after a long alienation. The precise expression remains necessarily vague, since language can really only approximate to the mystical experience through metaphors of rebirth. Cosmic mystery and individual destiny combine in a common presence.

In conclusion, I should point out that, unlike the struggles undertaken by most of the other heroes of this collection, Janine's experience has none of the lucidity of the Absurd hero. The actual discovery is, in fact, presented as the result of chance, thus underlining the purely individual, perhaps unrepeatable nature of the experience. Isolation from others remains total, for Janine wishes to be set free 'même si Marcel, même si les autres ne l'étaient jamais' (p.31): in short, this ephemeral union with nature is egotistical once again, as it invariably is in *L'Envers et l'Endroit*. The moment of fusion is clearly indebted to the description given in 'La Mort dans l'âme' (p.37), and at this extreme there is really neither choice nor explanation possible, hence no doubt Janine's cryptic reply to her husband: 'Ce n'est rien, mon chéri'.

The heroine's experience is complete in itself; that it cannot be indefinitely prolonged is the consciousness which exacerbates her exile. It is the permanence of such exile that the next story illustrates.

'Le Renégat ou un esprit confus'

With a brutality unparalleled elsewhere in Camus's *œuvre* the opening lines of this story thrust the reader into the heart of a text of exceptional violence consisting of the internal monologue of a brutalised 'renegade' missionary. They also present the main axes of the story: *bouillie* vs. order, a tongue cut out vs. a 'tongue' which rambles on madly, an indistinct *quelque chose/ quelqu'un* vs. a single violent certainty. These are the most prominent of the antitheses on which the text is constructed, and it is therefore these which will direct our analysis of the central thematic and metaphoric threads: we will look firstly at a vision of sun, fire, metal, of salt, geometry, order and sterility, of *langues* (language and tongue) twisted, mutilated and silenced; at the theme of desire for absolute domination, satisfied in the perverted pleasure of humiliation, of masochism masquerading as a lust for power. Then, via a spatial metaphor, we will examine the suggestion of doubt which partly undermines the professed perverted ideals.

In the 1940s Camus declared, 'il faut garder à la violence son caractère de rupture' (P2, p.1571) and, like *Caligula* or *La Chute*, 'Le Renégat' illustrates the consequences of this moral stance, for it is a violent text, a text on violence and on the violence perpetrated by a certain kind of writing. Its function as *rupture* in the collection will become increasingly clear.

With the exception of the last line, the text of this story is made up of the crazed and interminable outpourings of a defeated and dehumanised creature: as in *La Chute*, the hero is the sole source of all the information given; there are no external points of reference, however insecure, no temporal anchorage, however vague; no reasonable objective relations between the hero and the outside world or other people. In one of the many acts of violence perpetrated by the text the reader is imprisoned within a mad monologue of unverifiable validity (others, more obvious, include the shock felt at the sadism, the perverted use of Christian language and the Lord's Prayer, pp.49, 54, 57). Thus deprived of the points of reference to which he is accustomed the reader is at the mercy of the text, at the limits in many ways of what he finds readable. And yet, the story actually points to the fact that it is a conscious search for coherence, as the narrator looks for 'le mot juste' for example. This well-ordered text is less a stream-of-consciousness than a coherent *récit* drawn therefrom.

Radical in its function within *L'Exil et le Royaume*, as its extreme negative pole, 'Le Renégat' is also exceptional in the way the main elements are brutally at variance with the norms of the collection.

This is true, firstly, of the action, for we are presented with the 'degré zéro' of events in the present of the story: a man hiding for hours in the desert to ambush a missionary and suddenly, at the end of the story, either achieving or dreaming of achieving this aim only minutes before he is caught and beaten. Zero movement of this kind is a radical departure from the more conventional stories of the collection because it exploits a common short story structure (the detailed description of a few crisis hours) not to relate events but to explore a deranged mind as the harsh outside world into which the hero escapes reactivates memories of a violent past and exacerbates within

him a state of confusion. Movement in his day is, like that of
Meursault in his cell, rhythmed by the movement of the sun as
he lies imprisoned within its violence, announcing the beginning
of the day (p.41), marking the passing hours (p.43), under-
scoring its increasing intensity (pp.46, 52). The metaphor used to
evoke its climax recalls the hero's own tongueless mouth: 'je vois
le trou [que le soleil] fait [...], bouche comme la mienne volubile,
et qui vomit sans trêve des fleuves de flammes' (p.51).
Confusion, perhaps hallucination, finally overcomes him (p.52).

This therefore constitutes a second departure from the norm:
the violent function of the sun has been internalised by the hero
to such an extent that it dominates both the descriptive and
psychological aspects of his monologue, undoubtedly colouring
the reader's appreciation of the less extreme landscapes of 'La
Femme adultère' and 'L'Hôte', which are closer to Camus's
numerous evocations of the North African world. It generates
most of the harsh metaphors which dominate the text, based on
metal, flames and violent blows, and which give the renegade's
narration its exceptional brutality. He employs the same
elements in his evocation of both the setting and the actors.

The town is huddled in a 'cuvette' (p.44), its walls carved out
with pick-axes, crushed beneath 'le couvercle de ciel bleu dur
[...] au creux de ce bouclier blanc' (p.46); and the surrounding
hills loom menacingly, 'en arêtes coupantes comme du fer',
rising from a 'mer de cailloux bruns [...] brûlante de mille
miroirs hérissés de feux' (p.44). The natives have 'des yeux de
métal' or 'une main d'acier', their sorcerer wears 'une cuirasse
de perles [...] avec un masque de roseaux et de fil de fer', and
their idol is '[une] double tête de hache, [un] nez de fer tordu
comme un serpent' (p.49). Repeated beatings and sexual
violence form the basis of their ritual and gradually convert (or
rather pervert) the missionary until he has been won over to 'le
fétiche dont j'ai l'image gravée au fer dans le souvenir et
maintenant dans l'espérance' (p.51).

A single long paragraph overtly summarises the interminable
monotony of the violence within this claustral world and fuses
both past and present (pp.50-52).

Throughout, the insistent, obsessive theme is that of

domination, culminating in the mutilation of the hero; and here again the exceptional character of 'Le Renégat' is forefronted. He relives the ecstasy of thinking that death, as the final extreme of violence, is to be his final victory, a shortcut to the nothingness which his self-abasement seems constantly to solicit (p.54). Instead, a 'new' individual emerges who is devoted to his new master: until that point the text had multiplied terms of subjection, but with his conversion 'une jeune haine s'est mise debout un jour, en même temps que moi' (p.53) and, in a violent apotheosis like the one of which Clamence dreams, he will at last be crucified on a 'selle guerrière' (p.59).

Christianity is overthrown, to be replaced by a religion based on diametrically opposed values (p.54). The insistent use of terms already encountered in 'La Femme adultère', or which echo the title of the collection, underscores their central importance: *le maître, le seul seigneur, prisonnier de son royaume, son royaume visible* (p.54). The similarities are, however, no more than superficial, for this terminology is part of a lexicon of violence which belongs to an anti-world.

The exaltation evinced in such outbursts seeks to disguise the fact that, far from being the apodictic statement he would have us believe, his (new-found) faith is merely the mad reversal of his earlier beliefs. The account of his past provides further evidence of this, since both his childhood and his former religion are given crudely negative characteristics (p.40). His sole response to this world was a desire to flee, cleverly linked by the village priest to Catholicism and the warmth of the sun. His arrival at the seminary was seen in similar ironic, victorious terms.

Religion and the family are also linked in what is perhaps the central idea of the story: 'râ râ tuer son père, voilà ce qu'il faudrait', but since the father is already dead, 'pas de danger, au fait, qu'il se lance dans la mission' (this 'il' is psychologically revealing in that it confuses the *Je* of the son and the *Il* of the father he wishes to replace, by overthrowing him). His conclusion, 'Alors il ne reste qu'à tuer le missionnaire', proves that he sees Christianity as primarily a system of values, an order, a hierarchy; hence, from one's mission to kill the father to the killing of the 'missionary Father' the logic is impeccable, though mad, and his attack on Western values cleverly displayed. The attack effectively concentrates on the duplicity of Christianity, as the vocabulary shows: a convert is a 'victory', the mission is to win over through the strength of their gentleness (p.43) and, above all, through the power of words, whose purpose seems more to obfuscate than to enlighten: 'J'ai cru au curé, il me parlait du séminaire[...] Il me parlait d'un avenir et du soleil[...] le premier à m'en parler a été le vieux prêtre[...] depuis je rêvais sur son récit' (pp.40, 42). Indeed, one of the most salient features of this text is the display of religious terminology, and while perhaps unsurprising in a seminarist/missionary, it is also a forceful sign of the supposedly oral nature of the *récit* and an instrument of its twisted logic: 'La Femme adultère' or 'Les Muets', for example, may adopt a language suited to their protagonists; they do not actually focus on their language and its abuses, as is the case here.

Swayed by the evangelising eloquence, which constitutes the centre of his (seminary) world, the already dangerously exalted seminarist formulates it as his ideal, in a suggestive satire of the 'Church Militant' of Catholic terminology (p.43). Once his tongue has been cut out he is deprived of both the means and the message, yet the new 'tongue' inside his head actually continues the language of domination.[1] Manifestly, his pleasure in being the object of ridicule and humiliation during his seminary days was really the concretisation of that dream, because self-castigation is for the renegade an instrument of self-glorification. It is for this reason that he succumbs to the greater power of his new masters.[2] The references to tongue, lips and mouth which are so prominent throughout, and which are constantly reinforced by the many references to words, cries, screams and the incoherent 'râ râ', have formed a solid ground

[1] A psychological reading links (sexual) desire to imitate the sorcerer, the cutting out of the tongue and fears of castration. The ambiguity is prolonged in the soldier's reference to the new missionary: 'ils [lui] couperaient [...] ce qu'il pensait' (p.56).

[2] *Bouillie* symbolises the non-phallic to which he is reduced when forced to accept the *ordre* of his new masters. This parallels the ambiguity of a number of Clamence's statements, for instance 'en attendant la venue des maîtres et de leurs verges' (P1, p.1546).

for the language/tongue metonym and, from the point of view of the narrative, lend a feeling of oppressive inevitability to the ending: the mute, raving slave is *silenced*, thus bringing to an abrupt close a text on the violence of language perverted (p.60).

The outburst of violence at the end produces in the hero an intense pleasure, as the rhythm of his ecstatic litany suggests, interspersed with the climactic 'frappez au ventre, oui frappez [...] Ah! le mal, le mal qu'ils me font' (pp.58-59). Once again 'Le Renégat' underlines its character of transgression: in the ritualised sexual assaults by the sorcerer (p.51), the aggressively phallic nature of the fetish itself, the 'ordures [...] l'odeur de tanière' (p.48). This intensely erotic pleasure of his litany is reminiscent of the highly charged pages of 'Entre oui et non' which deal with the mother and the cat which devours its young (pp.27-28), and they can be interpreted as part of a continuing psychological struggle waged by Camus to overthrow the figures of domination and aggression. In the early stages of his imprisonment the renegade had been violently reduced to enslavement and immobility, and the immobility of his day explodes in violence as the slave becomes the 'maître entravé tout-puissant' (p.58). This oxymoron reflects the momentary fusion of master and slave which the earlier desire to kill the father/ missionary Father was also meant to effect. His conversion to the fetish is part of the same process (p.55).

The repetition of terms like *esclave*, *méchant*, *entravé* is given a further twist which serves to disguise a remarkable, because uncharacteristic, revelation: once the world has been reduced to 'des foules muettes aux pieds entravés' then, proclaims the renegade, 'je ne serai plus seul' (p.59). The hero suffers from the irreconcilable tension between conflicting desires: the solitude of domination and the solidarity of suffering, and the closing delirium twists the writing into a radical disruption, a restatement or re-instatement of the thematic antitheses on which the text is constructed, and which it had striven to exclude: innocence despite guilt, communion despite solitude, faith despite the Absurd, desire despite sterility.

This theme of violence or domination is certainly the central element of the story; and the violence of the (natural) world is a striking illustration of it, supported by a spatial metaphor which conveys the ineluctability of a claustral world: the town of Taghâza, '[au] nom de fer'.

Taghâza is situated more mythically than geographically, in a paragraph which seems to parody the pattern of the heroic quest voyage, until the hero finally reaches 'la frontière de la terre des noirs et du pays blanc' (p.44). It is at this frontier (of experience) that myth replaces reality, for this is clearly not the Algeria of *L'Envers et l'Endroit*, *Noces*, *La Peste*, not the plausible Algeria of 'La Femme adultère' or 'L'Hôte'; it is an imagined extreme in which coalesce the hostile elements which form the negative pole of Camus's world. Salt, whiteness and heat form its basis, reinforced here by two complementary lines, one circular and largely horizontal (*cuvette*, *creux*, *igloos cubiques*, *couvercle*), the other linear and primarily vertical (*murs droits*, *écailles*, *épées*, *bouclier*). For the deranged mind of the missionary, torn between opposing forces, this town becomes both an 'enfer blanc et brûlant' (p.45) and 'la ville de l'ordre'.[3]

Taghâza is a town founded in violence, a continuing symbol of violence which secretes daily a rigorously orchestrated brutality (p.51). Here, in a striking oxymoron, the polar terms heat/cold are fused: 'une froide cité torride' (p.46); they are no longer opposites but the extremes of the same violence, just as white/black fuse in 'esquimaux noirs [...] dans leurs igloos cubiques' (p.45). Thematic antitheses undergo an identical development: Europe/Africa, Christian/barbarian, good/evil, violence/mercy are gradually perceived less as opposites than as phases of an ineluctable fusion within 'le règne de la méchanceté [qui] était sans fissures' (p.54).

The characteristics of the North African world to which Camus's earlier fiction had accustomed his reader are clearly violated here, and as a pure creation of the sun's violence Taghâza symbolises the absolute exclusion of man from the natural world. The town embodies a rigid certainty, harshness and aggressive definiteness of a carceral world which is unified

---

[3] Space does not permit the further development here of the symbolic links between the Father figure (order, master, domination) and the image of the town ('ville de l'ordre', 'stérile'), '[au] nom de fer'/au nom du père.

primarily because it is isolated, rigorously regulated, self-sufficient (pp.46, 54), 'la ville stérile [...] séparée de la nature', where time is reduced to the monotonous repetition of evil (p.54).

The hero's assertiveness is not, however, without its own fissures: his monologue also articulates an antithetical theme, of doubt or hesitation, triggered off (or at least coloured by) a theme common to L'Envers et l'Endroit, 'La Femme adultère' and other texts, the theme of nostalgia. As Cryle has rightly emphasised (see 9), this text is less an example of retrospection (with the distance this would imply) than a reliving of the past when past and present experiences overlap (cf. pp.39-40, 42, 43, for example).

Yet it is precisely because this esprit confus is constantly trying to control the 'bouillie', the madness in his head, that other drives can surface within the disorganised spontaneity of the monologue, grouped around the term 'frais' which links the rifle he holds in the present and evening rain of the past, which also reflects a series of doubts about the real power of his present masters (pp.45-46) by linking traces of salt on their robes to traces of snails after the rain. It is these evocations which prepare the surprisingly lyrical passage on 'l'eau de la nuit', developing into an image of the moon as a 'froide vigne d'or' (p.52). In 'La Femme adultère' similar elements overcame the heroine's dry, knotted past (pp.27, 34), and the vocabulary used in this second story suggests a similar victory: the angular, sterile, sandy world would be washed away and deliquescence would lead to destruction of the forces of alienation (p.45).

In each instance, however, the reminiscences are countered by recourse to his present situation and his new masters (pp.43, 46). Yet this is sometimes ineffectual, for if rain and freshness are the key elements tied to his past, then their presence in the following contexts can imply their final victory: on the fetish and hate (p.53), on the rifle (p.43), on his mutilation (p.53).

This conflict between antagonistic worlds and values — waged within the body and mind, the surroundings and imagination of the hero — reaches a climax at the same moment as the present action of the story (p.58): the recurring 'ombre violette' is enough to weaken his excited, sterile violence, and the closing lines of the story introduce the possibility of a defeat as poignant as that which faced his puritanical forerunner Caligula (pp.59-60). His more childlike requests express perhaps another truth, but the intrusive terms *à nouveau*, *autrefois*, and the future tenses discreetly preempt any positive conclusions. Truth, innocence and happiness would seem to lie, once more, in the past and if, as some critics have suggested, this story is a picture of modern man in search of absolutes, then it reflects the acute despair engendered by the failure of this search. 'Cette nostalgie d'unité, cet appétit d'absolu' on which *Le Mythe de Sisyphe* is based (see P2, p.110) is given here a negative, destructive shape. The renegade can no more attain absolute certainty than he can reunite his splintered personality. His psychological confusion and his enslavement are the product of the intellectual terrorism of which he was the all too willing victim.

Consequently, few definite conclusions can be drawn from this text, beyond the fact that however much one's reading may become an effort to situate it within the norms of Camus's more widely read fiction, it succeeds in resisting such normalisation. In this it both demonstrates and reactivates its 'caractère de rupture'. As readers we cannot trust the monologue if 'la folie [l'] a pris à la langue'; we cannot trust his antithetical values if his psychology has revealed a continuing desire for domination and pleasure in humiliation; nor his nostalgia for a gentler, more fraternal world if he was, in fact, degenerate; nor his belief in the future domination of his masters if he has successfully created a *casus belli* in assassinating the French missionary. Finally, we cannot even be sure that he has actually killed anyone, if the typographical break and his 'Ce long, ce long rêve, je m'éveille' (p.59) are seen as introducing a break between his crazed imaginings and his continuing imprisonment.

Such uncertainty is a major part of the text, indeed a major theme, as is evident in two central textual confusions: that of the 'I' of the hero who tends to confuse his identity and past experiences with those of others, be it his father (p.40), Christ (p.55) or the sorcerer (p.60); and secondly, the temporal confusions which stud the text (see *12*). From the psychological point of view it is clear that the renegade's confused mental state explains the abolition of conventional temporal relations, and as a textual strategy it prevents our concluding. Similarly, the mixing of reality and hallucination, of dream and consciousness, has precluded any evaluation in which what is 'real' is more valid than what is 'imagined' ('Les mensonges', as Clamence quipped, 'ne mettent-ils pas finalement sur la voie de la vérité?'; P1, p.1537). In a reality experienced by the deranged subjective vision of the hero, it is the attempted distinction between imagined and external which has become spurious; parallels and antitheses are no more than 'words' of a mind desperate for order but floundering in a disorientating uncertainty. Description here is, quite overtly, the process by which the narrator thinks the world in his own image, and his monologue is permeated by the confusion created by the shifting voices in his mind (pp.50, 52, 53).

No tongue articulates his final request to the sorcerer (p.60); no words respond to or reject it. It is only one more violent gesture bringing his narrative to a close, just as the final sentence, outside the quotation marks, abruptly deprives this (un)spoken monologue of its oral status, forcing it into the sterility of silence after the violence of language. In this the renegade's world is not unlike the very different story which follows it in the collection, 'Les Muets': here language is once again seen as a power-struggle in which the hero is victim.

'Les Muets'

'Ouvriers français — les seuls auprès desquels je me sente bien, que j'ai envie de connaître et de "vivre". Ils sont comme moi' (*Carn.* II, p.35). This diary entry of 1942 reveals how personally implicated Camus felt in the world of the working class, and 'Les Muets' is a conscious attempt to write about one aspect of their lives: 'Je ne pouvais perdre de vue que de réussir à décrire une grève, ou plus exactement ses effets, dans un langage communicable est un travail fort délicat' (Camus in *27*, p.46). For this task Camus chose a conventionally realistic form which entails direct presentation of the central character, an explanatory résumé of past events and the more than usually detailed physical description of both characters and places. This material is conveyed in a language which is largely devoid of images and which, by adopting Yvars's viewpoint and limitations, approximates both lexically and syntactically to the language of the workers described. The action of the story takes only a working day, and the stages are clearly marked: setting the scene (pp.63-65), providing the economic and psychological background to the strike (pp.65, 56), introducing the present action (pp.68-70) which leads to two encounters between boss and workers (pp.71, 78-79). Dawn over the town and the sea opens the story, evening over the town and the sea closes it, and into a simple life of repetition and restricted space (in which the sea is the sole escape) is inserted the disturbance of a unique event.

The opening sequence, of Yvars cycling to work, is similar to the framework used in 'La Femme adultère' because the journey allows a suspension of the action during which a thematic line can be set out: here, dual linked themes of a long-term situation dominated by age and a present crisis coloured by a sense of defeat. Having one foot in the grave (pp.63-64) is the consequence of a life in which age cuts off the pleasures of the natural world and imprisons in a routine (p.64). Growing old (pp.64, 67, 76), aches and tiredness (pp.64, 67, 76, 78, 79) and a heavy heart (pp.65, 67, 71, 78) form a sombre *leitmotiv* which gradually shifts the main focus of the story from the question of the strike and return to work to the wider human predicament.

In the second stage the long-term economic problem is enclosed within a bracket (opening with 'Ce matin-là, il roulait[...]' (p.65), and closing with 'Mais ce matin, une fatigue[...]' (p.67)) which terminates the first part by explicitly linking age and defeat. The economic problem is factually precise: a decline in production, the fear of redundancy as a skilled job is discarded, resignation giving way to anger (p.66). The crisis was clearly the cause of the strike, but its escalation is provoked by the boss's infringement of another, quite different code: this code dictates the spontaneous reaction of the men to Lassalle's intransigence, discarded paternalism and unwarranted insults, 'un homme ne parle pas ainsi', 'il n'était pas un homme' (p.67).

'Etre un homme', 'savoir se faire respecter', 'C'est contraire à l'honneur': such expressions are part of a recurrent code in Camus's *œuvre* which is evidently linked to his Algerian working-class upbringing and to his famous 'castillanerie'.[4] As such, it may well reflect an attitude of defiance which is of proven importance in his ethic of revolt. No justification, no explanation is ever offered, however, although in human relations (in insensitivity towards women or blind opposition to authority for instance) it frequently engenders negative consequences, as it does in 'Les Muets': the workers are immediately and quite unintentionally blocked in a simple reaction of silence as they file past the foreman on their return to work, 'humiliés [...] furieux [...] mais de moins en moins capables de rompre [le silence]' (p.69), and silence soon comes to signify their dignity in the face of humiliation. Yet it becomes cruel and divisive when it obstructs compassion at Lassalle's obvious anguish when his daughter falls ill.

The third stage begins as the men silently resume work; and both the strike and the closed gates are momentarily forgotten as a long realistic descriptive passage follows their work, in a display of concrete, practical and technical terms covering both objects and actions. The paragraph ends with the intimation that the workshop is returning to normality (p.71) and at this juncture the action seems to be embarked upon the uneventful resumption of the community of work.

In reality, the conflict which forms the central action of this story is only now about to begin, as the next paragraph announces: from this moment 'Les Muets' follows a simple chronological narrative development, built around the silence with which the men face the boss, first in the workshop, then in his office and finally, more dramatically, in the workshop once again after his daughter has fallen ill. The silence of the men becomes an instrument of their struggle, and this is confirmed when the delegates oppose the boss in an open clash (p.74). The

[4] Cf. Camus's portrayal of 'ce code de la rue' in 'L'Eté à Alger', *Noces* pp.72-73.

later justification of their action ratifies their condemnation of his behaviour: 'on leur avait fermé la bouche [...] la colère et l'impuissance font parfois si mal qu'on ne peut même pas crier. Ils étaient des hommes, voilà tout' (p.75).

This *dialogue de sourds* is interrupted by the camaraderie of the lunch-break and a renewed focussing on the activities of the men (pp.74, 75); through this the earlier theme of age and tiredness is reintroduced (p.76). Recurring again twice before the end (pp.78, 79), this theme links the worker's pain to the child's sudden illness and the boss's suffering, as their common human predicament strikes them all. In marked contrast to their earlier rejection, the workers express quite unconsciously their concern for the child, and their physical awkwardness (contrasted with the grace and skill of their working gestures) underscores the inadequacy of their verbal response (p.77).

It is on this helplessness that the closing pages of the text concentrate, conveying their inability to express themselves: like the faintly ridiculous Céleste of *L'Etranger*, Yvars cannot get beyond the simple commonplace, once deprived of the (comforting) rigidity of automatic, ready-made formulae (like those used against Lassalle).

The second encounter between boss and workers is a repetition of the first, as the text makes quite clear (pp.71, 78), and it is these two moments which the narrative superimposes, for the repetition reveals the chasm which separates the two apparently similar events: the economic conflict of the first encounter is complicated or rendered irrelevant (depending on the reader's point of view) by the human crisis behind the second. That Camus's intention was to give primacy to the human over the politico-economic is in keeping with his pronouncements elsewhere; that he intended the human to dominate is clear from the choice of a child as victim, since this is a surer way to gain the reader's sympathy.[5]

The reaction of the workers does not change, once again highlighting their inability to find a satisfactory response, or to find one quickly enough, and thus laying bare the largely involuntary

[5] The original manuscript of 'Les Muets' had planned to introduce a less clear-cut event, paralysis of the boss; P1, p.2045.

nature of their reaction. Even the emphasis on their show of fraternity as they leave the workshop seems to suggest its defensive nature. The hero's final outburst, 'Ah! c'est de sa faute!' may well be correct, but it leaves the problem unresolved and has been made to appear irrelevant.

The human crisis has thus effectively clouded the economic issue, and by pushing illness, old age and death to the fore Camus has actually abandoned the specific plot of a return to work after a strike in favour of a theme more central to his writing.

Throughout this sequence of events the natural world has been used to convey the passage of time (pp.63, 73, 74, 77, 79, 80) in a story where there is in fact little action. Nature is also of relevance to the thematic reading, however, in so far as the references situate the story within a wider, natural rhythm via the play of light which punctuates the passing of time (pp.63, 71, 73, 74, 77): it is the objective correlative to the violence of youth and the gentleness of age (pp.64-65), but the contentment which evenings usually bring to Yvars is not expressed in the final paragraph; the phrase 'Il aurait voulu être jeune[...]' suggests that he is now hopelessly excluded from a natural world with which he has lived in harmony by the sudden irruption of a human crisis in which his response has been inadequate.

Yvars is thus excluded not only from a wider human community — which critics usually contrast with the solidarity of the workers — but from the happiness he had known in harmony with nature (p.65). As in 'La Femme adultère' the ending covers the hero's return to his family, but the account to his wife of the day's events is undermined by the revealingly nostalgic 'en lui tenant la main, comme aux premiers temps de leur mariage' (p.80). Once again, as in L'Envers et l'Endroit, happiness would entail the recapturing of past happiness, and the human problem has upset the balance of a life which had accepted the fact that the past is irretrievable. Concretely, forty now has become old age (Camus, of course, was born in 1913, this story written in 1955), and unlike the narrator of the earlier essays, the hero cannot abandon others by concentrating on nature, for he is no longer insulated by youth and emotional enthusiasms. Camus's 1953 essay 'Retour à Tipasa' is also built on this shift and the acknowledgement that, 'je ne pouvais, en effet, remonter le cours du temps, redonner au monde le visage que j'avais aimé' (P2, p.870).

'L'Hôte'

In this, the fourth story of the collection, the scene is set in the opening paragraph: an isolated school on a hillside, a difficult track, a vast snow-covered high plateau; wind and darkness, a heavy sky. By the end of the story the clouds have cleared and the sun opens up distant horizons, in an overt counterpoint to the human world which has begun to close in on the protagonist. This isolated world is more hostile to man than, for instance, the streets and market of 'La Femme adultère' which partly protected the heroine from the harshness of the surrounding desert. Yet it remains less extreme than the 'enfer blanc' of 'Le Renégat'. Here, the inhabitants have suffered from eight months of drought, made worse by their dire poverty, and they are now dependent on the grain ration distributed to those of their children who attend Daru's school.

'L'instituteur' Daru, 'le vieux gendarme' Balducci, 'un Arabe': the *dramatis personae* of the story are rapidly and schematically introduced, and their relationships immediately suggested (pp.85-86). What then follows is the account of these relationships or, more precisely, of the conflicts latent in them, and which are forcibly introduced into the world of the hero: between Balducci and the Arab, Daru and Balducci, Daru and the Arab; between the legal (gendarme and prisoner), the cultural (French gendarme and teacher) and the cultural/ political (French teacher and Arab peasant).

The story is a study of psychological attitudes within a given crisis, so I shall first look at the development of the relationships and the consequences of the hero's defensive attitude, then consider the role of nature in the story.

Once the men are assembled within the confined space of the schoolhouse the simple chronological recounting of their few hours together charts the gradual crumbling of Daru's freedom:

he becomes as imprisoned in his unwillingness to take sides as
the Arab who, throughout, seems to accept his status as
prisoner. The steady progression is enhanced by the fact that,
with but three exceptions, only the moments of contact are
recounted; elsewhere the passage of time is reduced to summary
(pp.92, 95, 96). Hence the evolution of the story is clearly
defined, and complements the dramatisation of the confined
space: the schoolroom becomes a stage on which the three
characters evolve and, in a series of stage directions, their
positions and movements are noted in detail.

This behavioristic description has two functions: firstly, it
anchors the story firmly in the tradition of realism, and although
shorn of most of its psychologising explanations it does include
contrasting terms such as *trôner* (in reference to the gendarme)
and *accroupi* (when referring to the prisoner) which are
obviously far from neutral; secondly, it has a narrative role:
after following for ten pages the movements, gestures and
abortive dialogue the text openly displays their significance in a
simple phrase, 'Il n'y avait plus rien à faire ni à préparer. Il
fallait regarder cet homme' (p.94). This reveals the deliberate
effort of the hero to avoid or, at the very least delay, the
inevitable contact with his unwelcome guest; it signifies
unwillingness, perhaps confrontation. The recurrent motif of
looks exchanged or withheld, introduced from the beginning of
the story, now becomes significant, both in relation to Daru
(pp.83, 86, 93) and to the prisoner (pp.87, 92): the contrast is
explicit for Daru looks at, but avoids exchanging looks, while
the Arab prisoner openly looks him in the eye. We are, however,
given no information to help us decide whether the prisoner is
acting from fear, interest or bewilderment.

Their first conversation is rhythmed by the same *leitmotiv*
(pp.94-95), and it is reintroduced once more in the last two paragraphs as they part, although this time with slightly more
information: 'sans comprendre', 'd'un air indécis', 'le cœur
serré' (pp.100-01). Here the introduction by the omniscient
narrator of 'le cœur serré' abolishes at a stroke the (psychological) distance which Daru had wished to maintain, illustrating
how movement, sight and physical proximity have been used as

the concretisation of the psychological estrangement.

This development is interspersed with three parentheses which add necessary material about the past and help penetrate the hero's motivation in a way which such behavioristic sequences clearly cannot. The first consists of a long flashback which conveys haphazardly information on the bad weather and the eight long months of drought (pp.83-85). In this way the climate is given great importance from the outset, an importance directly explained by the last line of the parenthesis which echoes the title of the collection: 'Mais Daru y était né. Partout ailleurs, il se sentait exilé' (p.85).

The second suspension of the narrative (pp.92-93) ties the day's events in the schoolroom into a wider perspective as the text provides information about Daru's past and his early reactions. Here again the closing lines echo the title words of both story and collection, in an explanatory comment (p.93), which suggests that the two men do actually share an essential community. This potential narrative direction could plausibly be developed, but immediate reality is less harmonious in the line actually followed since the return to the present ('Quand il se leva[...]') repeats the desire to remain uninvolved. This confirms the Daru-Arab relationship as a conflictual one, and it will be less easily disposed of than the rejection of Balducci's attempted identification of national, racial bonds.

The third parenthesis (pp.95-97) consists of the hero's reflections during the night which follows, and just as his personal reaction to the desert had given way to impersonal formulation (p.92), so his thoughts here are general, circumstantial, moving from 'cette présence' to merely 'une sorte de fraternité'. In this way Daru disguises and displaces his personal (negative) response to the present situation by voicing a (hostile) judgement on a general problem, thus leaving himself uninvolved.

If Daru is a willing outsider, therefore, these few hours are enough to shatter his ideal, because actions, however simple, are not neutral and do not protect from others. It was perhaps this instinctive knowledge of the meanings which actions convey which had prompted, for instance, the Arab's 'Pourquoi tu

manges avec moi?' (p.94). In the same way, the underlying code
by which Daru has lived and decided (already seen functioning
in 'Les Muets') also fails: Balducci has acknowledged 'Tu es
d'ici, tu es un homme' (p.91), and the *leitmotiv* of handing the
Arab over to French justice (pp.89, 98, 101) is both the action
which the hero cannot perform (as the emotionally charged 'fou
d'humiliation' stresses) and the action which causes the final
misunderstanding and subsequent judgement (p.101). This code
dictates once again a rigid attitude, finally excluding other
human needs and leading to solitude; indeed, the manuscript of
'L'Hôte' made the parallel with the other occurrences much
more forcefully: 'Je suis gendarme', says Balducci, 'et je sais
que tu me méprises un peu' (P1, p.2051).

For Daru the consequences are not only a loss of friendship
and the recognition of the failure of communication, but also his
own exile from the desert world.

From the schoolhouse on the hillside the plateau is seen as an
'immense étendue', snowcovered; to the South, in the distance,
a mountain range scarcely visible in the bad weather (p.84). This
is the same world as that into which Janine is introduced, grey,
heavy, inhospitable. Here, however, the description relays a
much harsher reality than that of Janine's somewhat romantic
vision of its nomadic inhabitants, a reality reminiscent of the
world and living conditions which Camus had described in his
1939 newspaper series 'Misère de la Kabylie' (P2, pp.891-959).
Indeed, the text repeats the point that this is not a hospitable
world (pp.85, 89, 92), and the image of the harsh, sterile and
inhuman desert is close to that of 'Le Renégat' and, like the
priest, Daru has chosen this country precisely because of its
harshness and poverty (p.85). Here, he too is a *seigneur*; elsewhere 'il se sentait *exilé*' (my italics).

The motivation for this highly conscious choice stems perhaps
from Camus's expression of the desire to achieve a state of
dénuement, liberating the individual from the ever-present
conflict between the permanence of the natural world and the
fleetingness of a human life which tries to cloak itself in a feeling
of belonging. Those characters given to retrospection, those
troubled by growing old or, more directly, by the fear of death,

are negative exemplars of this consciousness, whereas characters
like Meursault, Clamence, even Caligula reflect a conscious
process of dispossession: 'je suis avare de cette liberté qui
disparaît dès que commence l'excès des biens. Le plus grand des
luxes n'a jamais cessé de coïncider pour moi avec un certain
dénuement' (*L'Envers et l'Endroit*, Preface, p.18).

The imprisonment by snow, darkness and heavy sky is trans-
formed the next day (pp.97-98), and the march of the two men is
rhythmed by the sun (pp.99, 101) until, having released the
prisoner and returned to the schoolhouse, Daru's earlier exaltation (p.99) is replaced by a stunned sense of exclusion when he
encounters the threat scrawled on the blackboard: 'l'instituteur
regardait sans la voir la jeune lumière.[...] Dans ce vaste pays
qu'il avait tant aimé, il était seul' (p.101).

Numerous indications in the text have shown that Daru's
action towards his guest (refusal to take sides? rejection of
community? pure misanthropy? refusal to make any choice at
all?) had slowly left him feeling ill at ease within his own little
kingdom (pp.95, 96, 98); and this has been intertwined with his
markedly hostile reactions of anger (p.89), hostility and
irritation (p.95), fury (p.98) and impatience (p.101). The price
he pays for this voluntary rejection is, as the closing lines make
quite clear, the loss of his solitary communion with nature. Daru
has, as it were, paid the price for what Camus's ideal had,
unconsciously perhaps but inevitably, contained of egocen-
tricity: rejection of the human community is (now) *ipso facto*
exclusion also from that relationship with nature (p.101).

The solitude into which Daru has been thrust is of a very
different nature from the solitude he had chosen for himself in
his schoolhouse. It is both negative and alienating; and the
reason for this appears clearly in a comment by Camus in 1944:
'Quant à ce sentiment de solitude qu'on éprouve authentique-
ment, il vient peut-être de ce qu'on délaisse les hommes et qu'on
s'adresse à ce qui ne peut répondre, c'est-à-dire à soi-même ou à
quelque puissance inconnue. On est toujours seul quand on
déserte l'homme parce qu'il n'y a que l'homme qui puisse être le
compagnon de l'homme. Et on déserte l'homme quand on
s'égare dans les silences éternels' (P2, p.1670).

It is this lesson which the next story is to repeat.

'Jonas ou L'Artiste au travail'

'Jonas' is an exceptional story, even in a collection as varied as this: in its unique comic and ironic tone, in the bourgeois artistic milieu which it portrays, in its use of a narrative technique which, in order to recount a long passage of time, both summarises sequences of events and multiplies the use of iterative passages (that is, where one telling represents a number of similar occurrences). It is also exceptional thematically in that it is the only story of the collection in which the tensions experienced by the hero are not polarised between nature and people: the natural world exists merely as a subject for Jonas's painting, which at times he either cannot paint (p.133) or uses as a substitute (p.132). The tensions generated here arise exclusively from the two closely connected roles of the hero as artist and as husband/father, for the story consists of a simple account of the increasingly cramped living and working conditions of the hero who, through unfailing faith in his good fortune, finally overcomes the multiple obstacles he encounters.

The focus of the action is on shrinking space and time, as the text announces as soon as the hero has settled into his dual role (p.111). Paradoxically, the shrinking actually takes the form of a proliferation: of objects, paintings, dogs, cups, papers; of people, children, friends, admirers, critics, hangers-on; of activities, painting, conversations, lunches, letters, telephone-calls, appeals. Jonas thus lives time, or the lack of time, as a problem within his flat. He is swallowed up by demands which obliterate the order and meaning in his life and, in this, he is a typical Camus creation, highly conscious of the present and its irreplaceable richness but forced into an endless *fuite en avant*. Jonas, we are told, is 'toujours en retard, et toujours coupable' (p.124).

The introductory paragraphs, however, present a hero who, like Gide's Lafcadio or Sartre's Oreste, lives in a world of unreality: he is free, loved, protected, blessed by Fate, pampered by his lucky star. Having discovered painting and marriage by chance (p.108) he was quickly successful in both and, coincidentally, at about the same time (p.110). Effortless studies (p.107), painting (p.108), success, these clearly form an exceptional existence, and the hyperbole used to describe it echoes Clamence's self-portrait in *La Chute*. Here, however, humour tempers the irony throughout and, more importantly, the irony is always the narrator's, never that of the character. 'Cœur pur' like his wife, Jonas avoids the quicksands of introspection into which Clamence disappears.

The central narrative line begins when the narrator's account singles out the exiguity of the living space, and this should be read as a narrowing also of focus producing a unique text which creates a modern, though a little less painful, version of Clamence's *malconfort*. The early stages concentrate almost exclusively on the various ways the artist's flat and time are occupied, and the ground-plan of the flat and the numerous permutations form an essential ingredient in the story's humorous development (see *10*). Jonas is finally reduced to immobility, painted by an official painter, working on a State-commissioned painting, to be hung on a wall (p.127). His passivity, marked throughout the story by the repeated 'Ce sera comme vous voudrez' and 'Ça c'est une chance', emphasises his immobility within a whirlwind of ultimately useless activity. The more art becomes his *raison d'être* (pp.128, 130), the more his imprisonment is confirmed, and the less he actually paints (p.131). He has been reduced to helplessness, and the text's first dialogue highlights this by weaving yet another spatial pattern around Jonas, his wife and friend while the questions raised are simply passed from one to the other and the only question answered involves yet another move within the flat.

The period of total inaction into which the hero is forced actually heralds the final stages of the conflict between creation and success by a very untypical movement: Jonas's expression of a personal opinion which actually disagrees with both a review article and his dealer, and his sudden awareness that, 'pour la première fois, il était gêné par les gens' (p.133). Reduced to total inaction, the hero escapes into an artificial world of alcohol, cafés and debauchery, but such escape is at best a gesture, and

Jonas quickly recognises its true egoistic and defeatist nature (p.136). By making brilliant use of the exceptional height of the rooms (earlier stressed as a source of problems), he retreats into an *abri* or *soupente* in the highest corner of the hallway where, through isolation, meditation and patience, he rediscovers his star, his art and his attachment to others. In short, he seems to overcome his growing alienation, and the conflict involved is graphically expressed on his last canvas (p.142). It has been suggested that the hesitation between *solitaire* and *solidaire* can be resolved by reading into it both terms, in which case, as with the titles of the two collections, apparent opposites are reconciled.

The focus of the action of the story on space and time has neatly dramatised the depiction of what are, in fact, quite meaningless events, while the rather farcical and frantic character of the story complements the endless flow of humorous and satirical traits. The targets of Camus's irony, in the opening pages, include critics, Freudian psychoanalysis, publishers, Existentialism, middle-class culture-seekers, endless officialdom, artists and landlords (pp.105-13). After such a wide introductory series the irony concentrates on the world of art, those who live in it and, much more pointedly, those who live off it. Jonas's flat and its inmates thus become a microcosm of the Paris society which Camus loathed (see *29*).

The tone is rarely bitter, however, and the overtones of theatrical farce which permeate the text are enriched by colourful descriptions which turn the flat and the antics of the characters into playful metaphors: it is an 'aquarium vertical' in which people 'semblaient flotter comme des ludions'; then a 'cabinet des glaces'; finally a 'boîte à surprises' (p.114). And each of these is picked up later as a thread of the story: in Louise's 'visage de noyée', in Jonas seeing himself painted as he paints, and in his ingenious escape into a box suspended in mid-air. 'Jonas' the Jack-in-the-box is thus a playful text, and the difficulty (and ingenuity) some critics have had in linking Jonas and 'his' whale (see *20* for example) is perhaps one more joke — at their expense — since the text had, after all, given due warning: 'Les disciples de Jonas lui expliquaient longuement ce qu'il avait peint.[...] Jonas découvrait ainsi dans son œuvre [...] une foule de choses qu'il n'y avait pas mises'.[6]

Further evidence of this ironic tone is provided by the fact that Jonas's family — a central serious element and emotional anchor without which the hero is lost — does not escape humorous treatment (pp.110, 115, 116). But the most prominent figure in this merry-go-round is the hero's star, for this generates multiple puns in the text which, as B.T. Fitch has shown (*11*), prepare the ground for the final pun on *solitaire/ solidaire*, itself a pun which Camus used elsewhere (in *L'Express*, Oct. 1955, for instance). Puns, of course, call for more puns, and it is this further *fuite en avant* which allows Jonas to resist fossilisation, that is the tendency to turn the work into a work of art, a finished product. Once again the text points the way: 'Ce ne sont pas tes tableaux que j'aime, c'est ta peinture' (p.122).

Of course, the game is also serious: success was, for Camus, the cause of major conflicts (cf. P1, p.2062), and he made the point with a certain desperation in his Nobel Prize speech: 'Restez un artiste ou ayez honte de l'être, parlez ou taisez-vous, de toute manière vous serez condamné. Que faire d'autre, alors que de se fier à son étoile et continuer avec entêtement la marche aveugle, hésitante' (P2, p.1906).

Yet the dilemma is, no doubt, insoluble, because the irony to which he resorts in 'Jonas' is dependent for its impact on the ability of the reader to recognise it; in other words, he is dependent on a public which is largely made up of the sorts of people his text sets out to pillory. What, therefore, is the function of humour/irony in this story? It disguises or, at best, distances very serious issues, and the change of tone which accompanies the end of the story is evidence of this: the star cannot hide the pathos of an artist slowly driven into self-doubt and sterility by the excessive demands made upon him (and this, of course, is true of Camus's own life; see P1, p.2061-62).

Despite the many disclaimers in which Jonas presents his star as alone responsible for his talent and his success, his story is actually built around his attempts to *work*, as indeed the subtitle

[6] Readers using the 'Livre de Poche' edition of *L'Exil et le Royaume* should note that this is given as 'ce qu'ils avaient peint', p.117.

implies (pp.117, 124, 125-26, 131), until finally '[il] réfléchit au lieu de peindre' (p.132), 'il ne peignait plus' (p.133).

The struggle to gain time is the struggle to gain the freedom to create, linked here to the equally important theme of the mysterious struggle within the artist to follow and express his own aesthetic (pp.118, 119), and the term used here, 'peinait longuement', not only overtly contradicts the incredible ease with which Jonas is said to have succeeded, it also projects into the story the importance of the artist's search for self-expression. A letter to the poet René Char illustrates this primary concern: 'Plus je produis et moins je suis sûr. Sur le chemin où marche un artiste, la nuit tombe de plus en plus épaisse. Finalement, il meurt aveugle. Ma seule foi est que la lumière l'habite, au dedans, et qu'il ne peut la voir et qu'elle rayonne quand même. Mais comment en être sûr?' (P2, p.1746).

The text also makes explicit the links between Jonas, his children, and his painting, for the children are the immediate bond with 'le monde et les hommes' (p.125), both a life-force and the source of complex and fundamental riches (p.131). Abandoning his painting includes abandoning his family and, towards the end, it is Louise's 'visage détruit', not a direct desire to paint once more, which suddenly brings the hero back to reality (p.136). He is suddenly able to organise his space, his time and his relations with others and, in a simple reversal of the vocabulary of the earlier decline, sitting thinking becomes part of the process of renewal (p.138): 'Il fallait qu'il découvre ce qu'il n'avait pas encore compris clairement, bien qu'il l'eût toujours su.[...] Il devait se saisir enfin de ce secret qui n'était pas seulement celui de l'art'. As was the case in 'La Femme adultère' (and again, later, in 'La Pierre qui pousse'), the precise nature of the hero's discovery remains perhaps necessarily mysterious, indefinable; it involves the recognition of forces *within himself* as well as ties to both family and painting. The closing paragraphs of the story are saturated with the language of affection as Jonas effectively overcomes what had, till then, been seen as conflicting drives (p.141). Whereas Janine had abandoned others in order to find harmony in the desert night (p.34), Jonas fuses both (pp.141-42).

The final lines imply that his star is no longer sole responsible because his temporary collapse as his period of rebirth comes to fruition is diagnosed as overwork (p.142). Furthermore, his long-term situation, if projected beyond the concluding lines of the story, remains ambiguous: to what extent has he really overcome the tensions between 'peindre les hommes, et en même temps [...] vivre avec eux'? A 1945 *Carnet* entry suggests that the solution is not an easy one: 'Créer pour rejoindre les hommes? Mais peu à peu la création sépare de tous et nous rejette au loin sans l'ombre d'un amour' (*Carn.*II, p.143). The extreme nature of Jonas's solution heightens our doubts as to its validity: his *soupente* is similar to Daru's withdrawal into a monk-like existence, to that of the 'vieux aux pois' of *La Peste*, and it has been called the temptation of the anchoret, the desire to 'diminuer la surface qu'il offrait au monde et dormir jusqu'à ce que tout soit consommé' (*La Mort heureuse*, Gallimard, 1971, p.42). Few, if any Camus characters go to the extreme proposed at the end of *Le Malentendu*, and certainly not Jonas; yet their solutions *are* often disturbingly egocentric, their exile often self-imposed (cf. P2, p.1670). This is true of Jonas who is said, but not shown, to have accomplished a withdrawal which reunites him with others. Whereas his solution is, at best, extreme and, at worst, highly ambiguous, the last story of the collection is usually seen as presenting a much clearer and more optimistic illustration.

'La Pierre qui pousse'

The opening paragraphs of this story about a civil engineer arriving in a small Brazilian town to plan the construction of a dam are actually structured in two groups, as is revealed by their first words: 'La voiture' (paragraph 1), 'L'homme' (2 and 3), 'Mais de l'autre rive' (4); 'Le bac' (5), 'L'homme' (6 and 7), 'Mais les cris d'oiseaux' (8). In both cases the interruption introduced by 'Mais' follows a reference to the night sky, its 'étoiles embuées' (p.146) and 'étoiles exténuées' (p.149). This framework serves to situate the main protagonists, who are associated through a shared quality of size and power both by references to what is actually perceived and to what is imagined in the surrounding darkness: d'Arrast is a *colosse*, the river flexes its *longs muscles liquides*. Silence dominates the entire scene, broken only by the sounds of water and the chain which drags the pontoon across (against) the river (p.147). At this stage it is not the colossus, however, who struggles against the river (animated via zoomorphic images) but the mulatto and negro boatmen (pp.147, 148).

All these elements merge in the explicit metaphor of epic adventure which, through hyperbole, brings the opening sequence to a climax: they are surrounded by a river bank 'immense et farouche', a 'continent d'arbres', a 'mer végétale', afloat on a 'fleuve sauvage', being whirled along towards the unknown: 'comme si, toutes amarres rompues, ils abordaient une île dans les ténèbres, après des jours de navigation effrayée' (p.150). Their odyssey, it would seem, is about to lead them into their next adventure...

The narrative brings this epic tone to an abrupt close, however: 'A terre, on entendit enfin la voix des hommes' (para.9); and it will be reintroduced only at the end of the story. Individuation takes over from epic exaggeration as the next few lines provide the names of both the characters and the setting, details of the journey, the destination, the purpose and human dialogue (in the direct speech of d'Arrast, the engineer, and his driver, Socrate). Only the metaphor which likens the daylong drive to a 'longue, longue navigation' (p.151) and the descriptive note which closes these first pages (p.152) recall the hyperbolic elements of the opening paragraphs. The heroic struggle against a hostile river is soon humorously reduced to a figure of the inflated rhetoric of a welcoming dignitary (pp.153-54).

Water does nevertheless continue to dominate the story throughout, and it is this which we will examine first, before looking at the human world.

The text underlines firstly the apparent indistinguishability of the elements: the sky is *spongieux*, *humide*, the stars, *embuées*, 'nageaient encore dans le ciel humide' (p.149); over the forest hangs 'une odeur molle et sucrée' (p.150); the forest is *humide*, a *mer végétale*, the air is 'un souffle humide, tiède' (p.152).

This insistence on the omnipresence of water, on its power to permeate the surroundings, continues throughout the description of the hero's day: everything he sees is *détrempé*, human beings are perceived as *silhouettes mouillées*, shadowy *gauchos humides* (p.155); finally, the entire town is described as an island planted in the centre of the forest which is everywhere visible above the rooftops and where '[tombait] ... un voile d'eau fine que la forêt épaisse absorbait sans bruit, comme une énorme éponge' (p.154). D'Arrast's visit to the lower part of the town is similarly centred on the image of the river encroaching on, absorbing the land (p.157); river, forest and sea merge with sounds as the hero 'écoutait toujours ce grand bruit spacieux [...] et dont on ne pouvait dire s'il était fait du froissement des eaux ou des arbres' (p.159). This sound becomes a recurrent element in the story, found in each of the subsequent episodes (pp.165, 166, 168, 175, 187).

Everything is submerged in this world and the hero's visit to the aptly-named 'Jardin de la Fontaine' is accomplished beneath 'une pluie fine';[7] even the mythical, miraculous statue of Jesus 'est arrivée de la mer, en remontant le fleuve', and the pilgrims take away as relics bits of 'schiste humide'. In this is conveyed a possible explanation of the story's enigmatic title (p.161).

This visit also shows that the focus of the story is not on the practical purpose of d'Arrast's visit but lies elsewhere, as is already hinted at in his refusal to address his mind to the practical questions put to him (p.162).

The macumba ceremony constitutes the climax of his encounter with the natural world and is the major example of their possible interpenetration: in its European/African, pagan/Christian syncretism it forms an extreme (though temporary) instance of the reintegration of the human being into natural forces beyond himself. The elements are reminiscent of the story's opening episode (pp.168, 169), and as was the case during the river crossing, although d'Arrast is involved in the events he remains partly a spectator. The ritual, however, is

[7] Proof that all this is symbolic, rather than realistic, is to be found in Camus's *Carnets* account of his trip to Brazil, where rain is given much less importance. Cf. also 6.

described in a language which finally suggests a certain similarity in the transformations which overcome d'Arrast and the local townspeople: they lose their human characteristics (pp.172, 173) and, at length, the beautiful *Diane noire* (whose presence throughout the story is associated with the hero's unfulfilled wishes, cf. pp.159, 169, 174, 176) 'pouss[a] un étrange cri d'oiseau, perçant et pourtant mélodieux' (p.174). This contrasts with the much more brutal metamorphosis of the other participants, but the most significant feature of the episode lies in d'Arrast's transformation: 'Le dos toujours collé à la paroi, il ressemblait [...] à quelque dieu bestial et rassurant' (p.170). Quite unconsciously he also joins in the dancing until he collapses 'le long de la paroi [...], retenant une nausée' (p.173).

There is nothing human in these metamorphoses; they are as extreme as the rituals performed in 'Le Renégat', though here without any violence. D'Arrast still remains an outsider, however, and is finally forced to leave: he re-enters the confused external world (in which the now familiar elements reappear) and his feeling of exclusion is total (p.175). In an echo of the title of the collection the hero anticipates only exile or solitude, yet the text seems to propose a different, indistinct narrative possibility: 'Mais, à travers la nuit humide, [...] l'étrange cri d'oiseau blessé, poussé par la belle endormie, lui parvint encore' (p.176).

A key to the understanding of d'Arrast's experience at this moment — strongly expressed in terms like *nausée*, *écœurement*, *vomir* — lies in this passage from *Le Mythe de Sisyphe*: 'et voici l'étrangeté: s'apercevoir que le monde est "épais", entrevoir à quel point une pierre est étrangère, nous est irréductible, avec quelle intensité la nature, un paysage peut nous nier. Au fond de toute beauté gît quelque chose d'inhumain.[...] Le monde nous échappe puisqu'il redevient lui-même.[...] Ce malaise devant l'inhumanité de l'homme même, cette chute incalculable devant l'image de ce que nous sommes, cette "nausée" comme l'appelle un auteur de nos jours, c'est aussi l'absurde' (P2, pp.107-08). It is, for Camus, this essential moment of consciousness which gives entry into the experience of 'le sacré' which, to use Maurice Blanchot's words, is 'la présence immédiate [...] cette vie simple à fleur de terre qu'annonce René Char [...] la réalité de la présence sensible' (see *L'Entretien infini*, Gallimard 1969, p.51). The macumba can then be seen as a ritual performed by the community precisely as a means of providing entry into this fusion with the world.

D'Arrast is both attracted and repelled, charmed and nauseated by the reality into which he has been introduced: as with Janine, it is this natural world in its extreme *otherness* that the hero has to learn to accept; and this is also true, of course, of d'Arrast's reintegration into the human world, his rediscovery of human community.

Whereas the epic opening suggested mystery, massiveness, a trial of strength, the somewhat less epic line which dominates once the hero awakens in Iguape is couched in humorous, ironic tones, underlining weakness and chatter. The mock-theatrical takes over from the (mock-)epic, as the description of both the mayor and the judge underlines the incongruous elements (pp.153, 141, 160), and the account of their welcome plays upon its farcical exaggeration (p.152). It is their manipulation of a social façade, however, which is given most emphasis: the mayor's 'contemplation morne' is switched to a 'ravissant sourire' (p.153); the judge's 'voix fracassante' can suddenly become 'harmonieuse' (p.156); and the port commandant, 'un gros noir rieur' (p.157) can quickly resort to a 'ton impératif' (p.158). In each instance it is the power wielded by this group — who openly refer to themselves as 'les notables' (p.154) — which breaks through the façade as they exercise their 'rigueur souriante' (p.157). D'Arrast is thus kept at a distance throughout his contact with them, and when he later deserts their balcony to join 'le coq' it is, implicitly, this practice of superiority which he rejects (p.182). The precise description of the judge's house — fine baroque architecture containing only cane furniture and a brood of little children (pp.178-79) — functions as a metaphor of this social façade and the emptiness behind the power.

D'Arrast's relationship with the world of Socrate and 'le coq' is constructed in overt contrast to the distance felt elsewhere, the dominant terms being *sourire*, *rire chaleureux*, *épanoui*, and with 'le coq' the hero is won over by his openness (p.165). It is to this that he responds when he goes to 'le coq''s aid during the procession, abandoning the town's dignitaries 'sans s'excuser'.

However, just as the actions of the chief of police introduce a disruptive note into the welcoming chorus of the mayor and his associates, so the hostility of 'le coq''s brother signifies that, at the outset at least, d'Arrast is not welcome into their community once he tries to step into their private lives: only the authority of the port commandant opens the door to satisfy d'Arrast's curiosity (pp.158-59). Both of these conflictual situations are later defused by a shared meal, before the macumba (p.168) and before the procession (p.177).

We can conclude from this that in each human situation the relationship is reversible: it harbours a possible opposition which reflects the many antitheses at work within the text, those of Europe/Brazil, Christian procession/native macumba, dignitaries/poor Blacks, balcony/'bas quartier', a river to be dammed/a river submerging parts of the town... D'Arrast's visit to the grotto provides a central example: at first ignored by the pilgrims (pp.161-62) he then makes contact with 'le coq' and their conversation (which occupies the centre of the story) illustrates this process of reversibility on precisely the elements which will finally allow him a measure of integration: he has come to Brazil because in Europe (i) 'je n'ai pas trouvé ma place', (ii) 'quelqu'un allait mourir par ma faute', (iii) 'Il me semble que j'ai appelé' (p.166); and here in Brazil, thanks to 'le coq', he is offered 'la place vide' (p.187), having helped someone accomplish a vow made so that he would not die (p.164), having answered someone's call (pp.164, 165, 182-83).

D'Arrast spontaneously seals his friendship with 'le coq' by rushing to his aid during the procession, and the account of his leaving the balcony and running out into the crowd conveys both his rejection of the theatrical etiquette of the dignitaries and his commitment to 'le coq' as he struggles against the crowd. The metaphor of 'marée humaine' permits the linking as common obstacle of the river (at the beginning of the story) and the crowds (at the end).

The last five pages recount his efforts to help 'le coq', first by

comforting him, then by replacing him as carrier of the stone
which, St Christopher-like, he lifts 'presque sans effort' but
which, by the end, 'pesait douloureusement'. The last paragraph
is exclusively made up of physical detail until the psychological
and emotional liberation are signalled by an onrush of metaphors which echo the image of the hero presented at the
beginning (p.187). Heroic stature and mysterious joy combine to
reinsert the protagonist into a context similar to that of the first
pages, but the mythical, Promethean aura cannot disguise the
important fact that this stature has been attained through a very
human action, has been enacted on a simple human level, ful-
filled in a hut, not a church.

D'Arrast's choice seems to have ended his solitude and given
him fraternity and friendship, thus confirming the story's
anchorage in the human; and this can be contrasted with
Camus's original manuscript version in which he had adopted a
conventional mythical ending: 'Il charge la pierre dans une
longue barque et remonte le fleuve vers la forêt vierge où il
disparaît' (P1, p.2065). Eschewing such mythical vistas the text
of 'La Pierre qui pousse' concludes on a human note; and yet,
the elements which had formed the basis of the first paragraphs
— river sounds, darkness, silence, strength, d'Arrast as colossus
— are also dominant in the closing paragraphs (p.187). His
abortive fusion with the natural world on the night of the
macumba has prepared this reinsertion into a poor human
community and an existence in which things earlier seen as
obstacles to be overcome are now experienced as necessary
elements of his integration: with nature ('le bruit des eaux
l'emplissait'), and with others ("Assieds-toi avec nous"). Mock-
mythical and mock-theatrical both implied distance, resistance,
the implication that d'Arrast was no longer the centre of his own
life (he had fled Europe and 'avait envie de fuir' Brazil). His
sense of alienation disappears when the outside world, the
human community and his own reality fuse in a new acceptance;
and the story shows that, far from being antithetical, these three
terms can constitute both exile and kingdom, and those
characters in other stories who have chosen one at the expense of
the other two have either failed or experienced only partial and

ephemeral harmony. For d'Arrast, on the contrary, it is rebirth, a new beginning: 'il saluait, une fois de plus, la vie qui recommençait' (p.187).

'*L'Exil et le Royaume*' as collection

It may seem to be a truism to state that the stories of a collection have to be published in a certain order, yet the choice which governs this order cannot be accidental, and the study of it should, therefore, yield a certain amount of information (see 9). If we look across the stories schematically a distinctive feature of the collection emerges, namely that whatever aspect of a story one chooses to follow, no links are to be found across them all; diversity, not homogeneity, is the hallmark of the collection. Hence, any tentative patterns one might wish to extrapolate are partial and arbitrary, for the stories seem refractory to any plausible, comprehensive grouping. Yet, as a 1952 project note reveals, they were in fact conceived as an ensemble (P1, p.2038) and their common theme was exile.

In the published collection, whatever point of entry one takes, one or more of the stories, early or late in the collection, through statement or implication, will block one's progression towards a unified whole: in their different ways 'Le Renégat', 'Les Muets' and 'Jonas' are the most frequent points of disruption, as though the other, more lyrical texts reflected a uniform voice while these three display their otherness; 'Le Renégat' because of the violence, the exceptional internal monologue and the heavily metaphoric nature of the writing; 'Les Muets', on the contrary, because of its realism and the simplicity of both theme and language; and 'Jonas' because of the all-embracing nature of the irony and humour.

One's conclusion therefore has to be that these stories are, at best, only partly integrated on the level of the dominant theme of exile and do not give the impression that they move towards a synthesis in the final story, traversing a number of inter-dependent phases.

Their diversity, and the impression of inconclusiveness it generates, seems to be a direct aesthetic result of an attitude of ambivalence that the pre-war texts, in contrast, know nothing of. *Le Mythe de Sisyphe* suggests that Camus felt his philosophical stance to be valid for everyone, and his early heroes often display an almost inhuman purity and fixity of purpose, be it in the puritanical monomania of Caligula or the bloody and wilful singlemindedness of Martha (see also, on *L'Etranger*, P1, p.1928). The result was a long line of irreconcilable oppositional constructions: innocence/guilt, Absurd/Revolt, victims/ executioners.

The polemic which greeted *L'Homme révolté* and the increasingly violent confrontations developing in Algeria shattered Camus's intellectual certainties and left him stranded between those he could not respect (the Right) and those with whom he could not agree (the Left). The belligerent tone of much of his writing of the 50s is a consequence of this failure and subsequent isolation, and the theme of exile announced in his 1952 project note is a reflection thereof.

The basic obstacle to a satisfactory global classification of these stories would appear to lie in the uncertainty as to *what* is meant by the two terms, exile and kingdom. I shall therefore try to shed some light on this question by treating it from two angles, the thematic and the socio-political.

Uncertainty is clearly aggravated on the thematic level by the ambiguity evident when comparing the endings: if the natural world of the present constitutes the kingdom, does it include or necessarily exclude other people? If exclusion comes with age to Yvars, how does Janine succeed in stumbling upon a kingdom? If Daru has found a kingdom in which he can live, why do Janine's or d'Arrast's seem less permanent? Such questions could be multiplied endlessly (see *23*, p.228, where J. Cruickshank lists possible meanings), each interpretation then undermined by what occurs in another story. There are no *fixed* poles (for example: nature = kingdom, age = exile), for it is the function of these stories to highlight the basic ambiguity of the human experience. Any global pattern breaks down since links cannot be pursued beyond the limited experience of an individual character; all are exiled, but each is imprisoned within his own exile.

This restriction is further reinforced by the limitations of the dominant spatial images: the exclusion of characters, from nature for instance, can be represented, but the kingdom, or entry into the kingdom, can only be suggested. Moreover, the image of exile is itself ambiguous, for it implies exclusion *from* somewhere (and the motif of the journey is a frequent concretisation of this). But if this implies the possibility of a return, or even the existence of somewhere to return to, then it permits an optimism or an idealism which these stories do not justify. Exile here is, far more radically, exile *within*: within time, nature, age, society, work, race, other people. These have embodied the estrangement suffered by the characters, 'étranges citoyens du monde, *exilés dans leur propre patrie*' (P2, p.664, my italics). In short, exile is man's permanent state, social, psychological and metaphysical: 'dans un univers [...] privé d'illusions et de lumières, l'homme se sent un étranger. Cet exil est sans recours puisqu'il est privé des *souvenirs* d'une patrie perdue ou de *l'espoir* d'une terre promise' (P2, p.101, my italics). The subject of these stories is the confrontation between this reality and man's desire, and it underscores the unrealisable nature of Camus's ideal, that 'vie libre et nue que nous avons à *retrouver* pour *renaître* enfin'.

One common denominator has emerged — explicit in the case of Janine and d'Arrast, inferable from what we learn about most of the others — namely, that 'entering' the kingdom consists of a complex movement, outwards towards nature and/or others, and inwards to rediscover the Self. Janine, Jonas and d'Arrast exemplify this movement; as for the others, where the hero is unable to liberate himself from negative forces he cannot grasp the fullness of his present.

In short, these stories stress less what constitutes the kingdom (this belongs to the enigma of the individual life) than the conditions and obstacles which impede discovery. I feel it is for this reason that the theme of waiting looms large in all the stories (pp.19, 40-42, 65, 98, 138, 161), for it marks the threshold of their kingdom. The unwillingness to fill in what has only been outlined deprives these stories of any fixed, single meaning; each is very firmly anchored within its own framework, isolated as a purely individual case.

This seemingly pessimistic interpretation is corroborated by a simple statement of the author in his introduction to the collection (P1, p.2039): exile 'y est traité de six façons différentes'; the kingdom is referred to 'dans le titre'. In short, exile is the reality presented, kingdom the ideal aspired to and, at best, 'le royaume est dans l'exil, l'exil est un chemin vers le royaume et le royaume peut être l'exil' (*17*, p.130). There is thus little real effective opposition at work between the two poles and the title should no doubt be seen primarily as a pointer towards an ideal, the texts themselves expressing desire rather than achievement.

Exile is both man's existential dilemma and a symbol with an important social and political content: focussed sometimes on the relations between the hero and a racially alien world, in 'L'Hôte' on a hero who belongs to the country but is caught between the races which constitute its people, in 'Les Muets' and 'Jonas' on the man whose labour and skills are controlled by others, on the artist who is gradually alienated as he becomes increasingly part of the market.

For Janine or the missionary entering the alien world of the Algerian South, for d'Arrast entering the jungle of northern Brazil, the reception is naturally that reserved for the European, and the rigours of their journey begin the process of stripping them of the illusions they had harboured about this world: Janine's *malaise*, d'Arrast's *nausée* and the renegade's extreme *bouillie* are caused by the harsh, alien nature of the lands and their inhabitants.

The conflict which the hero/heroine undergoes is caused in part by the reaction to the outsider and, especially, by the ability of the local people not to 'see' the foreigner (pp.18, 24, 25, 161, 162). It has been said that this behaviour was, in fact, a deep-rooted racist attitude of the European towards native populations (see P. Nora, *Les Français d'Algérie*, Seuil 1961), and the way in which it is turned aggressively against them in return is well exemplified in the (non-)encounter between Marcel, Janine and the Arab soldier. When, on the other hand, the local inhabitants are forced to acknowledge the presence of the

European, their reaction can again be silently antagonistic, as is the case when d'Arrast expresses the desire to look inside a hut (p.158). This was for a long time, no doubt, the only weapon available to the local population in a colonial society, and Camus's political writings show his awareness of the potential violence which results from stripping a people of its voice, be it its history or its culture (see P2, p.1873).

Complicity in this state of affairs was inevitable, even for a liberal French Algerian, as the figure of Daru and the chain of events in 'L'Hôte' illustrate. For Camus, the teacher had always represented one of the positive aspects of colonialism (cf. for example, 'Misère de la Kabylie', P2, pp.921-22), yet as a teacher Daru represents a European culture whose aim in Algeria, since the 1890s, had been assimilation of the native population (a point made brutally obvious with the missionary of 'Le Renégat'). What actually constituted assimilation is therefore of importance here: for historians like B. Droz and E. Lever it is a euphemism covering 'une entreprise consciente de déstructuration de la société musulmane et de ses institutions traditionnelles' (*24*, p.21). Assimilation necessarily meant deculturation, and the rivers of France chalked on the blackboard of an isolated country school are a telling symbol of it: France is the metropolis and knowledge is knowledge about France. For this reason, the 'sentence' scrawled over the blackboard, however 'malhabile', is in fact an eloquent condemnation, in the language of the oppressor, of the oppressor's language. Daru is condemned for not recognising his involvement, because he is isolated *from the outset* as the representative of a colonial system (cf. *13*, p.9), and definitively excluded from an Algeria in which — whatever he did or did not do — there was no longer a place for the Frenchman.

Daru's 'humanisme colonial' (*26*, p.266) is rendered inoperative and the extreme of this reality is displayed in the renegade's rampant will to power: that the guilty figure here is a missionary is probably the continuation of the ideological debate between priest and doctor, *salut* and *santé*, opened in *La Peste*. The values they defend are diametrically opposed and the priest's language of absolutes is condemned as the vehicle of illusion and domination. The breakdown in communication which the renegade's mad monologue represents is an extreme, but a wide network of elements can be linked to it: Janine's ignorance of Arabic, the boss's peremptory dismissals, Daru's unwilling conversation...

The need for clear communication was an imperative in everything that Camus wrote, and the splintered perspectives and ambiguity of this collection highlight the difficulty of achieving it: whether via the surface incoherence of internal monologue or the surface limpidity of social realism there develops an awareness that it is not just the language of the law (*L'Etranger*) or bureaucracy (*La Peste*) which is divisive, which ensnares; all language separates (individuals, classes, races) unless it is the language of the senses.

The figure of Marcel is a concrete example of this problem, because the traditional realism of his portrayal renders him more transparent than the renegade, while the paucity of psychological information encourages the reader to see in him less an individual than a type. Together these factors combine to produce an illustration of the automatisms by which oppression is perpetuated: Marcel belongs not to the hated 'colon' class, but to that of workers and shop-keepers (see P2, p.973 and *24*, p.40); however mediocre he may appear, 'La Femme adultère' reveals his (supposed) superiority as a European (pp.17, 19, 20, 23, 24), firmly anchored in his biased opinion about the Arabs (p.21). His direct statements (pp.23, 24) are reinforced by textual mechanisms: the couple are presented as knowing no Arabic, yet the driver's use of it provokes a depreciative *pérorer*, and spoken all around Janine it is categorised as 'de cris gutturaux' (p.19). Such reactions are a clear indication of a balance of power which, even in the banality of everyday life, gives Marcel his status (in his own eyes, at the very least), and Janine's comment, 'elle aimait son courage à vivre, qu'il partageait avec les Français de ce pays' (where the generalisation is no doubt imputable to the narrator) is clear approbation of this state of affairs.

This attitude cannot be said to be exempt from racial consciousness; indeed, to demand anything else of Camus would be naive or tainted with bad faith. But to deny or minimise this content is equally invalid (see *9*, p.58 and *16*, p.58), for these stories do indeed reproduce some of the patterns of the relations at work between cultures.

Exclusion is the consequence of such racial antagonism, and it is also a central theme in the overtly economic or productive conflicts on which 'Les Muets' and 'Jonas' concentrate.

The historical process seems less abrupt here, but no less irrevocable: economic change is slowly pushing aside the coopers, and the specific conflict is a consequence of this (p.65), for in a shrinking market the bosses are openly dominant ('C'était à prendre ou à laisser') and their mask of paternalism is replaced by openly hostile gestures (p.68). Defeated when they try to resist, the workers are deprived of the ability to voice their opinion and silence becomes their last weapon. To oppose, as some critics have, human fraternity and class solidarity (in the name of the former) is to ignore the fact that the economic injustice which the boss perpetuates has already effectively excluded him from the wider fraternity which the workers share (p.64).

It is true, nevertheless, that Yvars's 'Ah! c'est de sa faute' merely prolongs the chain reaction of cause and effet, aggression and counter-aggression and, whether taken politically or humanly, acknowledges rather pessimistically man's imprisonment, cut off from happiness in both the natural world and the human community.

For many critics this dead-end is overcome in the final story by d'Arrast's integration into the poor black community after his rejection of the dignitaries, yet class and cultural divisions clearly remain. Such pessimism in the depiction of social relations is the politically dominant note in these stories, if one recognises the repeated inability of their heroes to find a response which would enable them to develop *within* their society.

'Jonas' is the final aspect of this sense and process of alienation: as an artist the hero needs to cut himself off from others in order to produce (and in this he is contrasted with the social aspect of the work of Daru, d'Arrast or, especially, the coopers). Yet his success as a painter is alienating because the market turns his paintings into products for sale by a '*marchand* de tableaux', turns his freedom to create into underpaid work (pp.106, 127, 132). While formally Camus has relinquished here the obvious social realism used in 'Les Muets' in favour of a theatrical, ironic text, his story emphasises the view that painting is production: in the subtitle 'l'artiste au travail', in the terms *travaux, travail, effort, travail acharné*. His work is, however, no more valid than the increasingly unwanted skills of Yvars: in both cases the work is alienating since it is, for both, part of the process which is cutting them off from an activity which had given their lives both structure and meaning.

The final irony of 'Jonas' lies in the fact that the process of alienation is not merely a central theme but is actually at work through the text: in 1953 Camus admitted that his *œuvre* (and fame) had become a prison: 'Depuis quelques années [...] mon œuvre ne m'a pas libéré, elle m'a asservi' (P1, p.2062).

Conclusion

'Il est difficile de revenir sur les lieux du bonheur et de la jeunesse. Les jeunes filles en fleur rient et jacassent éternellement devant la mer, mais celui qui les contemple perd peu à peu le droit de les aimer.[...] Cette mélancolie est celle de Proust' (P2, p.670); it is also Camus's (see P1, p.2037), and it is the sentiment which dominates *L'Exil et le Royaume*, colouring the depiction of lost paradises. Only the renegade escapes, since his choice had always been that of hell; yet even he knows the nostalgia bred of exclusion. In this the stories reveal a lasting fidelity, as the works of the intervening years indicate if we look over them from the point of view of the conclusions we reached concerning *L'Envers et l'Endroit*. In each case we shall first recall the theme, then point briefly to its development in later texts, and finally summarise its workings in *L'Exil et le Royaume*, singling out both changes and similarities.

The early texts had been based on a love of life which was given intellectual validity and moral weight by being centred on a constant awareness of the reality of death; yet the irruption of death into the individual's world effectively shatters the happiness of Caligula, Maria, Meursault or the group in *La Peste*. It is either abetted, resisted or fully accepted; but death in *L'Exil et le Royaume* no longer adds the intellectual spice to the spontaneous energy and vitality valued by the narrator of *L'Envers et l'Endroit*. Indeed, it can cause enough fear to dictate an entire life, or else its inevitability increases the heaviness and sense of defeat in everyday life. It thus actually alienates the individual from the love of freedom in nature which it had so enhanced earlier.

If, as R. Quilliot has suggested (P1, p.2037), *Le Premier Homme* was to present 'un homme sans passé', therefore innocent, then *L'Exil et le Royaume* was perhaps the necessary *tabula rasa* before the 'pèlerinage aux sources que voulait être *Le Premier Homme*' (P1, p.2039); in which case the collection is less a conclusion attempting to balance exile and harmony than a transitional, negative phase.

As the analysis of *L'Envers et l'Endroit* revealed, the present is lived with the greatest intensity in the experience of the suspension of time which accompanies moments of fusion with the natural world. Nature was seen primarily as permanence, cyclic return, stasis; and when excluded from it (in *Caligula*, *Le Malentendu* or *La Peste*) the individual experiences a violent disruption of the balance of life that, in *L'Etranger*, initiates an internal quest which, through the estrangement imposed by prison life, leads the hero (back) to the values which constitute happiness. *La Chute* here is the anti-*Etranger*, perpetuating a divorce from happiness and innocence. In *L'Exil et le Royaume* happiness has the diversity of life: it can be discovered in the natural world or among other people; it can lie in the past while the present conveys a feeling of exclusion; it can be achieved accidentally or after a long apprenticeship, by a sudden decision which interrupts a conscious need to flee. With the exception of the renegade, none was always exiled or will be permanently happy: the world, others, the past or the present, spontaneity or hyperconsciousness, all these are now ground for both exile and happiness. The oscillation between the two (in story and collection) is evidence of the abiding tension in Camus's vision, a tension which *L'Envers et l'Endroit* had concentrated upon.

Finally, we saw how lucidity had gradually replaced happiness as the professed aim of the narrator of *L'Envers et l'Endroit*; and in the major works that followed various doses of the same two ingredients reappear, but only in *L'Etranger* does lucidity actually lead to happiness. It now no longer needs the external pedagogue of *Caligula* or *La Peste* to bring consciousness; it can bypass the mental sophistication of a Clamence. Now, an impression, a desire, or an event is sufficient to uncover 'la face blême de l'inquiétude'; and what this development loses in dramatic impact it gains in subversive effect, because it is in the consciousness of the absurd limits to an individual, everyday existence that the anguish of exile is revealed. In this, no doubt, lies Camus's final faithfulness to the world of *L'Envers et l'Endroit*, 'ce monde de pauvreté et de lumière où j'ai longtemps vécu [...] cette vieille femme, une mère silencieuse, la pauvreté, la lumière' (pp.13, 25). The short stories are closer in form and content to the anecdotes and descriptive vignettes of *L'Envers et l'Endroit* than any of the other works, dominated by brilliantly simplified mythical figures, and the thematic balance of the two texts is remarkably similar: in both the *envers/exil* is dominant, while the *endroit/royaume* looms large as the exceptional moment which justifies the long acceptance of the un-exceptional. In both, such moments are rare. In both, the antithetical structure gradually reveals the fact that the ideal is achievable only when the antitheses themselves merge, when the character discovers that exile and harmony are the two inter-dependent faces of the same reality. The novelty in *L'Exil et le Royaume* lies mainly in Camus's recognition that such 'faithfulness', far from necessitating a choice, can actually be inherent in simply living one's life; that far from striking only the old or the exceptional, it can erupt at any time in ordinary lives.

Camus's response in the face of such a lesson is to reassert a passionate belief which already infuses his first texts: '"Il n'y a pas d'amour de vivre sans désespoir de vivre"[...] Je ne savais pas à l'époque à quel point je disais vrai; je n'avais pas encore traversé les temps du vrai désespoir. Ces temps sont venus et ils ont pu tout détruire en moi sauf justement l'appétit désordonné de vivre. Je souffre encore de cette passion à la fois féconde et destructrice'. With these lines, written in 1954 (for the preface to the republication of *L'Envers et l'Endroit*), Camus shows quite clearly that he has come full circle, that the stories of *L'Exil et le Royaume* express the same fears and rework the same quest as that first published collection, *L'Envers et l'Endroit*. The distinctly less complacent tone of the short stories might suggest, however, that he is (perhaps inevitably) moving further away from a lost paradise: the circle takes him not back to his origins but to the threshold of the spot which marks their absence.

Select Bibliography

Place of publication is Paris unless otherwise stated.

A. EDITIONS OF CAMUS'S WORK

L'Envers et l'Endroit, Collection Idées (Gallimard, 1970)
L'Exil et le Royaume, Collection Folio (Gallimard, 1972)
Théâtre, Récits, Nouvelles, Bibliothèque de la Pléiade (Gallimard, 1967)
Essais, Bibliothèque de la Pléiade (Gallimard, 1965)
Carnets,I: 1935-1942 (Gallimard, 1962)
Carnets,II: 1942-1951 (Gallimard, 1964)
Cahiers Albert Camus, I: *La Mort heureuse* (Gallimard, 1971)
Cahiers Albert Camus, II: *Le Premier Camus* (Gallimard, 1973)

B. CRITICAL STUDIES ON L'ENVERS ET L'ENDROIT

1. Dermenghem, E., *'L'Envers et l'Endroit* d'Albert Camus', *Les Cahiers du Sud*, 198 (oct. 1937), 604-07
2. Gothot, C., 'Les essais méditerranéens d'Albert Camus', *Marche Romane*, IX, 2-3 (1959), 59-74 and 113-32
3. De Luppé, R., 'La source unique d'Albert Camus', *La Table Ronde*, 146 (fév. 1960), 30-40
4. Valgny, J., *'L'Envers et l'Endroit* par Albert Camus', *Livres et Lectures*, 124 (juill. 1958), 395
5. Weiss, M., *The Lyrical Essays of Albert Camus* (Quebec, Naaman, 1976)

C. CRITICAL STUDIES ON L'EXIL ET LE ROYAUME

6. Castro-Ségovia, J., 'L'Image des réalités afro-brésiliennes dans "La Pierre qui pousse"', *Présence francophone*, 1 (aut. 1970), 57-69
7. Conilh, J., 'L'Exil sans royaume', *Esprit*, 26e année, 260 (avril-mai 1958), 529-43 and 673-92
8. Cryle, P., 'Camus nouvelliste: *L'Exil et le Royaume*', *La Revue des Lettres Modernes, A. Camus*, 6 (1973), 7-19
9. ——, *Bilan critique: 'L'Exil et le Royaume' d'Albert Camus* (Lettres Modernes, 1973)
10. Curtis, J.-L., 'Structure and space in Camus's "Jonas"', *Modern Fiction Studies*, XXII, 4 (1976), 571-76
11. Fitch, B.T., '"Jonas", ou la production d'une étoile', *La Revue des Lettres Modernes, A. Camus*, 6 (1973), 51-65

12. Johnson, P.J., *Camus et Robbe-Grillet. Structures et techniques narratives dans 'Le Renégat' et 'Le Voyeur'* (Nizet, 1972)
13. Kessous, El Aziz, 'Albert Camus et l'honneur de l'homme', *Simoun*, 31 (1960) 3-12
14. Lekehal, A., 'Aspects du paysage algérien, étude du fantastique dans une nouvelle d'Albert Camus, "Le Renégat"', *Cahiers Algériens de Littérature Comparée*, 3e année, 3 (1968) 15-32
15. Olivier, P., *'L'Exil et le Royaume* d'Albert Camus', *Le Divan*, 303 (juill. 1957), 190
16. Perrine, L., 'Camus's "The Guest", a subtle and difficult story', *Studies in Short Fiction*, I,i (Fall 1964), 52-58
17. Picon, G., 'Albert Camus: *L'Exil et le Royaume*', *Mercure de France*, 1125 (mai 1957), 127-31
18. Thoorens, L., *'L'Exil et le Royaume'*, *La Revue Générale Belge*, 93 (mai 1957), 155-56
19. Vigée, C., 'L'Errance entre l'exil et le royaume', *La Table Ronde*, 146 (fév. 1960), 120-26
20. Wetzel, H., 'Commerce métaphorique: de *Moby Dick* à "Jonas"', *L'Arc*, 41 (1970), 63-71

D. GENERAL AND CRITICAL STUDIES

21. Clayton, A.J., *Les Etapes d'un itinéraire spirituel* (Lettres Modernes, 1971)
22. Costes, A., *Albert Camus ou la parole manquante* (Payot, 1973)
23. Cruickshank, J., *The Novelist as Philosopher* (London, Oxford University Press, 1962)
24. Droz, B., and E. Lever, *Histoire de la guerre d'Algérie 1954-1962* (Seuil, 1982)
25. Gassin, J., 'Fils et mère chez Camus: aux origines d'un lien exceptionnel', *La Revue des Lettres Modernes, A. Camus*, 5 (1972), 271-73
26. Girardet, R., *L'Idée coloniale en France, 1871-1962* (Livre de Poche, 1979)
27. Grenier, R., *Albert Camus (Souvenirs)* (Gallimard, 1968)
28. Lazere, D., *The Unique Creation of Albert Camus* (New Haven, Yale University Press, 1973)
29. Lottman, H., *Albert Camus: a biography* (London, Picador, 1981)
30. Nicolas, A., *Une Philosophie de l'existence* (P.U.F., 1964)
31. Quilliot, R., *La Mer et les prisons* (Gallimard, 1956)

CRITICAL GUIDES TO FRENCH TEXTS

edited by
Roger Little, Wolfgang van Emden, David Williams